Cacti
and
Succulents

Cacti
and
Succulents

Graham Charles

The Crowood Press

First published in 2003 by
The Crowood Press Ltd
Ramsbury, Marlborough
Wiltshire SN8 2HR

www.crowood.com

British Library Cataloguing-in-Publication Data
A catalogue record for this book is available from the British Library.

ISBN 1 86126 610 3

Dedication
To my wonderful wife Elisabeth for her love and understanding. I have so
enjoyed sharing our interest in plants ever since the moment we met.

Acknowledgements
Sharing with others is a vital part of any activity and so it is with growing
cacti and succulents. I am indebted to all the people over the years who
have encouraged me and taught me, my companions on the many visits to
see the plants in their habitats and the many I have met who have become
my friends. I am particularly grateful to everyone who has helped me with
this book by allowing me to photograph their plants or by providing
pictures. Here I must make special mention of Tom Jenkins, the British
Society's Chairman, who introduced me to the project and gave me support,
advice and pictures, particularly of other succulents. Also my good friend
Chris Pugh, whose companionship, growing skills and commercial nursery
are a constant inspiration. Another excellent grower is Bryan Goody, the
owner of Southfields nursery, who allowed me to photograph some of his
wonderful plants for this book. Then there are my generous friends who
loaned me their photographs: Derek Bowdery, Eddie Cheetham, Eddie
Harris, Tom Jenkins, John Pilbeam, Albert and Daphne Pritchard, Chris
Rogerson and Bill Weightman – a big thank you to all of them. Finally,
a special thank you to my wife Elisabeth for her support and for proof
reading the text.

Photographic Acknowledgements
The names of picture contributors will be found in the captions. All others
are by the author.

Frontispiece: Mature plantings of succulents at the Huntington Botanical
Gardens, California, USA.

Designed and typeset by Focus Publishing, 11a St Botolph's Road,
Sevenoaks, Kent TN13 3AJ

Printed and bound in China by Bookbuilders

Contents

Preface

It was just over forty years ago when, as a young boy, some friends of my parents gave me my first cacti. My father was a keen gardener and encouraged me to take an interest in plants. It was not long before my expanding collection took over his greenhouse, ousting his tomato plants. As far as I remember he was philosophical about it and continued to support my interest. We saw an advert for the local branch of what was then the National Cactus and Succulent Society, so he took me to the next meeting and we joined that evening. With the encouragement of the other members my interest grew rapidly and I think it has continued to grow ever since, some would say to obsessive proportions! It is certainly true to say that I have derived great pleasure from the hobby, moving my interest from one plant group to another, one aspect of the hobby to another, meeting kind and genuine people, many of whom have become my friends.

The world is very different for young people today. There are so many exciting things to do that you might think that cultivating something as slow growing as a cactus would not appeal any more, but in fact children still find them fascinating and are a major proportion of the buyers at garden centres. Gardening in general is ever more popular; and conservatories, which are becoming more common than previously, make an ideal environment for many succulents. They fit in with a hectic lifestyle, since they have no objection to being left without water for a while and they don't grow too quickly, so you can spend time with them when it suits you. When I had a demanding career, I used to find the time in the glasshouse a perfect opportunity to relax – after all, nothing happens quickly in a succulent collection!

My aim in writing this book is to give any reader an insight into what the hobby is really like today. I have tried to explain what makes it so much fun and how satisfying it can be. There are no long, wordy descriptions of the plants, just the features that make each one special and what you need to know to get the best out of them. The illustrations are more informative than any description ever can be. The Latin plant names may be a bit daunting but people soon get used to them. Unfortunately, botanists tend to change the names, so I have used the latest ones and referred to older ones you may still encounter. The advice and recommendations are based on my own experiences and may not always agree with what was written years ago and copied ever since. If you are new to the hobby, then I hope you will find all you need in these pages to get started. If you already have an interest in cacti and succulents, then there will be further stimulus for you here. I have given references to other books and sources of information to enable you to develop your hobby further.

Good growing!

Graham Charles
Stamford, UK 2003

1 The Unique Nature of Succulents

Evolution and Adaptation

What are succulents and how do they differ from other plants? There is no absolute definition of a succulent, it is a case of degree – some plants are extremely succulent and others only slightly. Not everyone agrees and succulent collections often contain plants that are only marginally succulent. It is not just a case of storing water; to be a succulent a plant must have evolved ways to conserve its reserves. Some plants, such as begonias, have stems full of water but they are not succulent since they soon wilt and die in a prolonged drought. Succulence takes a number of forms depending on where the water is stored; for instance, there is leaf succulence where the leaves are enlarged with water-storing tissues such as is seen in echeveria and mesembryanthemums. These leaves can exhibit modifications to reduce transpirational loss of water such as a covering of hair or a waxy bloom.

Stem succulents have thick stems where the water is stored and this is the strategy of most cacti and euphorbias. Stem succulents such as pachypodiums and some euphorbias have normal leaves that grow when water is available and shed in times of drought. Other succulents store water underground in swollen roots, an effective strategy in extremely arid places. In fact, the big swollen subterranean or surface storage may not be roots at all but an adapted part of the stem, for which the term caudex is often used. By combining different types of succulence a plant can be particularly effective at storing water during periods of prolonged aridity.

Lithops otzeniana, *a leaf succulent that mimics the stones amongst which it lives.*

Obvious examples of stem succulents are cacti, euphorbias and stapeliads, which usually have green stems because they have taken over the function of photosynthesis from the leaves, which are often absent or greatly reduced. In some cacti such as epiphyllums and schlumbergeras, the stem has become flattened and looks like a leaf. Where true leaves are present, they are shed at times of drought. The stems are usually ribbed or tuberculate to allow for expansion and contraction without damage as water is absorbed or lost. In cultivation, splitting can still

Some leaf succulents like this Haworthia maughanii *have evolved windows in the tops of the leaves to allow photosynthesis within.*

Many cactus-like euphorbias such as this E. ingens
have leaves that are lost during the first dry spell.

occur due to excess water being given, particularly after a long dry period. Spherical or cylindrical stems are the best shapes to minimize surface area for a given volume.

A remarkable difference between most succulents and other plants is in the photosynthetic process they use to manufacture sugars. Normal plants have green leaves that contain chlorophyll and this is where photosynthesis takes place. Salts and water from the roots are combined by light energy from the sun with carbon dioxide from the air to make sugars. For this to happen, the carbon dioxide must be able

*Stem succulents from
Africa in the genus
euphorbia (centre and
left) look a lot like the
New World cacti
(right), but they do not
have areoles, which are
only found on cacti.*

to enter the leaf through pores in the surface called stomata that open during the day. Oxygen, which is produced as a by-product of the process, subsequently escapes through these open stomata. Evaporation of water also takes place through the open stomata, which is no problem to a normal plant since it can be replaced from the roots, but for a succulent this loss would reduce its ability to withstand drought. The solution adopted by most succulents is to open their stomata at night when the evaporation loss will be greatly reduced in the cool night air of their natural habitats. They achieve this by fixing the carbon dioxide taken in at night with organic acids that then break down into carbon dioxide and water during the hours of light to be available for photosynthesis. This adaptation was first observed in a member of the *Crassulaceae* family and is therefore known as Crassulacean Acid Metabolism (CAM). It is for this reason that greenhouse vents should be left open at night in summer to allow the temperature to drop enough for this process to work effectively, and why many cacti do not grow well when planted in tropical places where the night temperature regularly exceeds 20°C (68°F).

The most common confusion is between true cacti and other succulents. What is the difference and how can you tell them apart? It is clear from the above that cacti are one example of succulent plants. The strategy of evolving succulence as a way of coping with long dry periods can be found in many plant families. In some, only a few genera or even a few species are succulent; while in others, all the genera are succulent. The cactus family (*Cactaceae*) is one of the latter; every cactus is a succulent. So how do you decide if a plant belongs to the cactus family? There is no simple way since plants from other plant families have evolved to cope with the same environmental conditions in the same way as cacti and hence look very like them. In fact, they look so alike that experts can sometimes be fooled so there is no need to be concerned if you have difficulty differentiating them. However, there are a few characteristics that, if taken together, can confirm that a plant belongs to the family *Cactaceae*. They all have spines, even though in some species they are greatly reduced and difficult to see; and they all have areoles, the structures from which the spines grow. These look rather like pincushions but can be very small and difficult to see in many species.

All cacti are from North and South America although they have been introduced to other continents where they have become naturalized so that they look like they belong there. The reason they are only found naturally in the New World is that they evolved after the landmass that became South America drifted away from Africa (part of Gondwanaland). Later, when South America moved northwards it came close enough to North America to allow cacti to migrate and evolve into the wealth of species found today in Mexico and the USA. Of course if you see plants in cultivation you will not know where they grow naturally so you depend on characteristics you can see. Cacti are most easily confused with the succulent euphorbias from Africa, which through parallel evolution have grown to look very like cacti. Look closely and you will see that euphorbias do not have areoles. Another obvious difference is in the flowers, which are small and usually insignificant in euphorbias but larger in cacti. With practice, the differences become more obvious but there are a few genera of cacti that look very different from the classic image. For instance, the primitive cactus genus pereskia has large leaves,

Pereskia grandifolia, a true cactus, has large leaves and flowers that look like a rose.

Some cacti like this opuntia have leaves that only appear on the new growth. Note the areoles.

Cacti often have large bright flowers like this Thelocactus heterochromus, which also has prominent areoles from which the spines and flowers grow.

Seedlings of cacti (two trays in foreground) are very like those of other succulents – euphorbia (back left) and hoodia (back right).

thin stems and flowers that are quite reminiscent of roses, hardly what you would expect for a cactus, but they still have areoles. The various pictures in this book should provide the beginnings of an understanding of this dilemma and experience of cultivating plants will eventually make you wonder why you ever confused them.

Flowering

Euphorbias often have small and insignificant flowers. Some species such as E. obesa are dioecious: the female plant is on the left, the male on the right.

There is a commonly held perception that cacti do not flower, or that they do so only every seven years. The correct treatment of cacti is widely misunderstood, which might explain why well-grown plants are so rarely seen anywhere other than in specialist collections. All cacti and succulents are flowering plants – as

long as their requirements are satisfied then they will flower, sometimes spectacularly, but always beautifully. Other than the correct cultural treatment, the only other criterion for flowering is maturity. Once a plant flowers for the first time it is mature and will flower every year thereafter, so long as the environmental conditions are right. Even in the natural habitat conditions may be unfavourable, for instance, a plant may miss a year with its flowering if there has been no rain. Not all individuals of the same species will flower at the same age; there are slight genetic differences that mean some will reach maturity before others. Rarely, a particular specimen may grow perfectly well, but for some reason will not flower, even though it is older and larger then others of the species that do so reliably. There are a few species that just will not flower in cultivation in northern Europe, either because of insufficient sunlight, or because they need to be extremely large before they are mature. However, they can still be valued for their architectural appearance.

Flowers of most cacti are short-lived, sometimes just a few hours, depending on the

Many species of matucana have flowers evolved for pollination by humming-birds.

The flowers of Grusonia invicta *open in the day for pollination by flying insects such as bees.*

Weberbauerocereus longicomus *has large white flowers that open at night and smell musty to appeal to bats that pollinate them.*

weather and the species. They are produced from the areoles of the cactus and in species such as some rhipsalis and eriosyce, a single areole can produce a number of flowers, either simultaneously or in succession. The plants lose significantly more water when flowering than they do normally, and sometimes you can see the plant has shrivelled after its blooms have been open on a hot day. Some have evolved the ability to set seeds without actually opening their flowers, a phenomenon called cleistogamy. Frailea, for instance, are small plants that can ill-afford to lose moisture so they will only open their flowers when they are well watered and turgid, otherwise they rely on cleistogamy. This is less of a problem for the many night-flowering cacti whose flowers lose less water in the cool of the night. Healthy plants that are growing well flower the most but there is an interesting exception. If a specimen loses its roots and dehydrates it sometimes produces more flowers than normal, presumably in a last effort to reproduce. A similar effect can be observed when a cutting that is dehydrating before it has rooted unexpectedly flowers, sometimes even when the plant it was cut from has never obliged.

A remarkable phenomenon that you can observe in your glasshouse is the ability of plants of the same species to flower simultaneously. Even if the plants have been obtained from different sources, a large proportion will flower on the same day. Whatever the mechanism for this behaviour, it is remarkably accurate. It can often be observed in habitat as well.

The flower diversity in other succulents is even greater than in cacti, reflecting the floral characteristics of the many plant families to which they belong. These are discussed in Chapter 5.

Pollination

Many cacti are self-compatible or self-fertile, which means that a single plant is capable of setting seed, either without any help from a pol-

Discocactus *have sweet-smelling, nocturnal flowers with a long narrow tube for pollination by moths.*

linator or by the transfer of its own pollen from stamens to stigma. However, most species are self-incompatible, so the pollen needs to be transferred by an insect, bird or animal from the stamens of a flower on one plant to the stigma of a flower on a different individual of the same

species. Some flowers are unselective and are pollinated by a range of creatures, but there are also interesting flowers that have evolved to appeal to specific pollinators. The pollination syndrome was once used to separate genera but in today's classification a single genus may contain species which have unselective flowers as well as those adapted for a specific pollinator. For instance, mammillaria has a few species, once called cochemiea, which have humming bird flowers and a similar situation occurs in eriosyce.

Flowers that are rotate and open in the day can be pollinated by flying insects, notably bees, flies, wasps or even beetles. The other group of day flowers has evolved to appeal to hummingbirds; and these are usually red, sometimes yellow or green, and unscented. The flowers can be bell-shaped, like some echinocereus and lobivia; tubular, like some cleistocactus and melocactus; or zygomorphic, like schlumbergera.

Night-blooming flowers depend principally on pollination by bats or moths, but the flowers often stay open for some time the following morning, so giving other creatures a chance to contribute to effective pollination. Flowers pollinated by bats are bell- or funnel-shaped, usually pale-coloured inside, with thick fleshy petals to enable the bat to cling on. They have large numbers of stamens with copious pollen, and usually smell unpleasant to humans. The genera with this sort of flower are the large arborescent cerei such as carnegiea, pachycereus and weberbauerocereus. Finally, moth-pollinated flowers are smaller with copious nectar at the base of a very long, thin flower tube into which the moth can extend its proboscis, sometimes to more than 20cm (8in). They have white inner petals, a strong sweet perfume, and can be found in diverse genera such as epiphyllum, pymaeocereus and discocactus.

The Cephalium

An interesting feature of some cacti when they reach flowering maturity is the formation of a special growth used only for flowering. This highly adapted structure is called a cephalium and it takes many different forms. It is mainly the columnar-growing cerei that have cephalia,

The cephalium on espostoa can extend from the growing point for more than 2m (6.5ft) down the stem and flowers can be produced anywhere along its length.

which appear as a woolly or bristly growth, usually down one side of the stem, and originating from the apex. These sometimes sit in a deep groove and can distort the shape of the stem. A good example of this form is espostoa in which the cephalium can extend for more than 2m (6.5ft) down the stem. Nocturnal flowers appear from the cephalium, followed by the fruits, which are expelled from the cephalium when ripe. Another form, only seen in arrojadoa and stephanocereus, is where the cephalium grows as a clump of bristles in the growing point, and then a normal vegetative shoot grows through it, leaving it behind like a collar. Flowers are then produced from these old cephalia for many years (*see* page 73). Finally, there are the terminal cephalia that appear in the growing point of the plant when it matures. Once this begins, the production of normal vegetative areoles ceases, so that only the cephalium grows, as in the genus melocactus.

When the cephalium starts to grow on a melocactus, like this M. bellavistensis, *the green part of the body never gets any bigger although the cephalium grows ever taller.*

Classification and Nomenclature

Unlike many other popular plants, most cacti in cultivation are true species rather than hybrids. The only cacti that have been hybridized to any great extent are epiphyllums

Many Brazilian cerei have cephalia like this Micranthocereus dolichospermaticus, *which only grows on isolated rock outcrops.*

(the so-called 'orchid cacti'), echinopsis and astrophytums. Because of this, plants are usually known by their botanical names rather than a common or cultivar name. This can be daunting for beginners but it is surprising how soon the Latin names become familiar. The *Cactaceae* family has been divided into around 100 genera, and it is the genus that forms the first name of the plant. Each genus has a number of species belonging to it, and it is the species that forms the second name. Some species have been further divided into sub-species (or varieties, which used to be the preferred division). Perhaps because cacti have little commercial value, their classification was mainly the province of amateurs during the twentieth century when most of the species were discovered and named. This resulted in many minor variants being given their own species name (the so-called 'splitter's approach') to a much greater degree than would be the case in other plant families.

There have been many notable attempts to classify the cactus family over the years, either as a whole or by individual genera. At the end of the nineteenth century, cactus exploration and writing was dominated by Germans, the most famous contemporary publication being Schumann's monograph *Gesamtbeschreibung der Kakteen*. The first major work in English, *The Cactaceae* by Britton and Rose, was published between 1919 and 1923 and remains a landmark in cactus literature, the first edition being beautifully illustrated with colour plates. The most extensive and influential work of the century was *Die Cactaceae* by Curt Backeberg. Published between 1958 and 1962, Backeberg's 'splitter's' view became the popular approach for thirty years. This was reinforced by the appearance of his lexicon in 1966 that summarized the contents of Backeberg's monograph and was translated into English with additions in 1977. This remains the most complete treatment on cacti to this day even though many of the plants that Backeberg accepted are now considered to be synonyms of others.

More recently, botanists have endeavoured to reduce the number of recognized species by combining a number of those originally described into broader concepts of species. This has also happened with genera, which has resulted in the disappearance of familiar and much-loved names such as notocactus, neoporteria and lobivia. The new consensus was arrived at through consultation with specialists around the world, and the results of their deliberations were published in 1999 in the second edition of the *Cactaceae Checklist*. This process of rationalization, which is still evolving, will culminate in a new English-language cactus lexicon, scheduled for publication in 2004.

It has to be said that this has not been popular with hobbyists who like to have a name for every variant in their collections. A specialist collector could now find that his extensive collection of a genus, which represents dozens of wild populations with corresponding names, is now combined into just two or three species. Similarly, the new genera that are botanically defined now encompass plants that are very different from a collector's point of view, perhaps including tree-sized species and true miniatures.

The story of the nomenclature and classification of other succulents is similar to that of cacti with most being discovered and described in the nineteenth and twentieth centuries. The task of producing a comprehensive book about succulents fell to Hermann Jacobsen, curator of Kiel Botanic Gardens in Germany, and author of *Handbuch der Sukkulenten Pflanzen* published in 1954, followed in 1960 by the *Handbook of Succulent Plants*, an English-language edition. A lexicon appeared some years later, first in German then in English translation. This summarized and updated the contents of the *Handbook*, and remains a useful publication today. Published in 2001-3, the six volumes of *The Illustrated Handbook of Succulent Plants* are a comprehensive and up-to-date treatment covering 9,000 taxa, the only problem being the high cost.

History

Succulents from southern Africa first came to Europe at the beginning of the seventeenth century following the colonization of the region. During the eighteenth century, explorations of the interior yielded a steady stream of new discoveries that reached a peak around the end of the century when large numbers of mesembryanthemums were introduced. The names of the explorers will be familiar to succulent enthusiasts because of the plants they found and those named after them. Francis Masson, working for Kew Gardens, introduced the most living plants of any collector. He wrote and beautifully illustrated *Stapeliae Novae*. William Burchell spent four years travelling in South Africa during which time he amassed 50,000 botanical specimens. The first

Schumann; Britton and Rose; Backeberg and Ritter – authors of the major cactus works of the twentieth century.

reference to lithops may be found in his book *Travels in the interior of Southern Africa*

Cacti were probably first brought back to Europe from the New World at the beginning of the sixteenth century and they gradually started to appear in accounts and illustrations. They caused much interest because of their peculiar appearance, but unfortunately these early specimens came from the West Indies and were much more difficult to cultivate than those that would be found later. It was not until the end of the seventeenth century that there were enough known species to start to differentiate genera, the first four being cereus, opuntia, pereskia and melocactus. In the middle of the eighteenth century, Linnaeus introduced the idea of plant binomials and applied them to the twenty-two species of cacti he recognized. From the early nineteenth century onwards the number of species in cultivation increased rapidly. This was partly because of the explorations of plant hunters, often working for the European botanical gardens, and also as a result of the development of proper glasshouses.

If the historical aspects of succulents fascinate you, a wonderful and well-illustrated book entitled *A History of Succulents* by Gordon Rowley provides a comprehensive and entertaining account of all aspects of the subject

An early engraving of cacti and succulents published in the Florilegia of De Bry in 1612.

Uses

Although the indigenous populations of the natural habitats of cacti and succulents have found many uses for them, there have not been any applications that could be said to make them economically important. There were attempts to use the sap of euphorbia to make rubber and the manufacture of sisal rope from agave leaves is quite a big business, but none of the diverse uses of succulents have ever been important enough to attract much attention from professional botanists. Those that have been involved have worked on them through a personal interest in the plants.

Cacti are represented in ancient pottery, such as that from the early Peruvian civilizations, where alkaloids found in the sap of the San Pedro cactus were of great ritualistic importance. The ceremonial use of peyote in Mexico is also of ancient origin – the collectors removing just the heads so that the plant can regenerate from its tuberous roots. Agave sap has long been used to make pulque, an alcoholic drink that was consumed with peyote in ceremonies. The sap of some agaves can also be fermented to make tequila, a fashionable drink available worldwide.

Beneficial drugs have been made from succulents, such as a heart stimulant obtained from the flowers of *Selenicereus grandiflorus*, and the steroid diosgenin extracted from the caudex of dioscorea for the manufacture of cortisone. Perhaps the best-known aloe is *Aloe vera*, for which many medicinal properties have been claimed, the sap being an additive to many health products. The sap of other aloes also has medicinal applications such as that of *A. arborescens*, which can be used to treat burns. The sap of some euphorbias has been used as an ointment.

Cacti and some succulents are used by farmers to make hedges or fences. Cuttings of columnar cacti are placed in a line and when they root they make a very effective fence. Opuntias and agaves are used in a similar way but can become a pest if they spread into the surrounding countryside. The dried stems of

Church doors made from the wood of Echinopsis pasacana *in northern Argentina.*

some large columnar cacti are suitable for building material. *Echinopsis pasacana* is used in this way in northern Argentina since there are no trees for the local people to use for making roofs and furniture. The resin from the bark of the dragon tree, *Draecena draco*, is used in cosmetics and varnishes.

Many cactus fruits may be eaten, in fact the fruits of hylocereus can even be found in European supermarkets. Opuntias also produce edible fruits so long as you remove the spines. Other uses for opuntias include cattle fodder, a spineless hybrid having been produced for this purpose; and as a host for the cochineal insect, a sort of scale, which is the source of the dyestuff cochineal, used as a red dye for centuries and in recent years for the manufacture of lipstick.

Choosing Species to Grow

Chapters 4 and 5 describe and illustrate a selection of cacti and succulents which are well suited to cultivation under glass even if some will eventually get too large. The total number of species known exceeds 10,000, so it is not

possible to cover such a large range comprehensively in a book like this. The plants included have been chosen either because they are the most attractive of their kind and are currently popular with growers, or they are reasonably easy to obtain either as seed or young plants. Some of the more difficult to cultivate species are included because the challenge of growing them well is part of their attraction. Such a small selection is bound to omit plants which are well worth growing, so there are references to specialist literature, which should be consulted to find information on a wider range of species in the various genera. For full details of this further reading, see Appendix III.

The cacti are organised by the classification published in the 2nd edition of the 'CITES Cactaceae Checklist', the most recent attempt to reach an international consensus on the nomenclature of the *Cactaceae*. Nomenclature from older books may not use the same plant names and some of these old names are still in regular use, so a plant may be found with a different name from that used here. To help avoid confusion, commonly used alternative names are mentioned in the text. *A New Cactus Lexicon*, based on the same nomenclature as this book, and illustrating most of the 2000 accepted species and subspecies is in preparation and will be published in 2004. It is expected to become the comprehensive reference for identification but will not include other aspects of the hobby such as cultivation. The nomenclature used for the succulents is based on that from the most recent books published on the various families.

Cacti

The cactus pages are organised alphabetically by generic name, except for 'Columnar Cacti' which is a selection of popular tall-growing plants from various genera, and 'Mexican Treasures' where you will find a collection of choice slow-growing plants.

Other Succulents

The succulent pages are organized by alphabetical order of plant families so that similar plants will be found together, except for 'Miscellaneous Succulents', which is a selection of plants from other families.

2 Succulents in their Natural Habitats

All the continents of the world have arid areas and, except those that are completely dry, all have plants adapted to live there. Succulence has evolved in many plant families as a strategy to cope with periods of drought, so succulents can be found in many of these dry places but those of most interest to the collector are from North America, South America and Africa. It is a common belief that these plants are only found in deserts, which are technically places that receive an annual rainfall of less than 25.5cm (10in). Of course, many do live in these places, but succulents can also be found in a range of different types of habitat such as grasslands,

forests and high-altitude plains. The annual rainfall of an area is not the only thing that determines whether succulents will flourish. The important thing is when the rainfall occurs and hence how long the dry periods last. If there is regularly no rain for months then plants must adopt a strategy to cope with this, therefore succulents from such places have evolved to store large reserves of water. Those from regions with shorter droughts will need less storage and are therefore often less succulent.

The climate also determines what other plants grow in a locality. Succulents are not capable of surviving competition from leafy plants that over-

The Sonoran desert near Tucson, Arizona, one of the easiest places to view cacti in habitat.

Neobuxbaumia make spectacular forests in Mexico. Photo: Derek Bowdery

Yucca brevifolia and ferocactus in the Mojave desert, USA.

niche have no leaves, many species have developed flat leaf-like stems to increase their surface area for photosynthesis in their shady environment. This is particularly apparent in epiphyllum, which means 'upon a leaf', referring to the flowers that appear to grow out of leaves.

Altiplano is the name given to extensive areas of high-altitude plains, located mainly in the tropical regions of the Andes. Approximately 4,000m (13,000ft) above sea level, the altiplano is home to many cacti. Resembling European moorland with no trees, just low bushes, it is extremely cold during winter nights. In this unlikely habitat the cacti keep near to the ground, many developing thickened roots for water storage, whilst others form low hummocks in a similar way to many alpine plants. This strategy enables the plant to enjoy the microclimate near the ground, avoiding the bitter winds that frequently blow over this harsh landscape. Further south, away from the tropics, a comparable habitat can be found at lower altitudes in Patagonia where the plants have made similar adaptations. In some places these plants can be covered with snow for months, hardly what you would expect for cacti, but then there can be long periods of drought when their succulence ensures their survival.

grow them, so in an area receiving regular rainfall, these other plants will generally predominate. However, even in these places, succulents can find niches where the competition is less, such as rock outcrops or where the soil is too shallow for the other plants to grow. Examples of this can be found in Brazil where various cacti are found on rock outcrops in the forest, some even adapted to only grow on one type of rock.

A particularly interesting habitat adaptation has evolved in cacti that live as epiphytes such as rhipsalis, epiphyllum and schlumbergera. These live on the branches of trees or sometimes rocks in the same way as many orchids. Their roots grow in the leaf litter that accumulates on the branches, simply using the tree as a perch to get nearer the light in dense woodland where the canopy of trees makes the forest floor too dark. Since the cacti that inhabit this ecological

The massive Stenocereus weberi *in Oaxaco, Mexico.* Photo: Derek Bowdery

Aloe africana *and* Euphorbia polygona *on Robin's Hill, South Africa.* Photo: Daphne Pritchard

Conophytum meyeri *on a quartz hill near Uitspanpoort, South Africa.* Photo: Chris Rodgerson

The greatest concentration of succulents is found in Africa, particularly southern Africa. Most of the huge number of mesembryanthemums may be found here, including lithops, the famous 'stone plants' that look like the rocks among which they grow. Most of the popular euphorbias, aloes, crassulas, stapeliads and other choice genera also come from this region, which may be divided into a number of rainfall zones, both in terms of quantity and season of occurrence, each with its endemic species. In many places succulents are the predominant vegetation although many species are very small and so not immediately obvious, particularly those that have evolved to mimic their surroundings.

Visiting the Plants in their Natural Environments

For the enthusiast, the chance to see these plants in their natural environment is hard to resist. But bear in mind that once you have been, you will never feel quite the same way about your plants in pots again, nor are you likely to be satisfied

19

In the USA, there are many national parks where the plants have been protected and can be seen in their natural state. Outside the parks, pressure of human activity, particularly ranching, has restricted the plants to a few undisturbed places and the private fenced land should not be visited without permission. Particularly recommended for seeing cacti are Anza Borrego Desert State Park, California; Saguaro National Monument, Tucson, Arizona and Big Bend National Park, Texas. There is plenty to see in these and many other national parks in the south-west USA and there are usually local guide books available to help you identify the plants you see, so for a first experience this a safe and easy way to enjoy a succulent habitat. Another way is to go on a trip organized by a tour company or one of the cactus societies. These are usually quite expensive, but everything is organized for you, so there is no need to worry about car hire, where to stay or where to go to see the plants. This is a particular advantage if you don't speak the local language.

Spectacular large clusters of Copiapoa dealbata *near the coast in northern Chile.*

to go only once. There is always another hill to explore or another plant to find! If you get the opportunity, the easiest regions to visit are the USA, mainly for cacti, and South Africa for succulents. If you go to the right places you are guaranteed to see spectacular succulent landscapes.

Echinopsis korethroides, *growing at high altitude in northern Argentina, makes large clumps of stems.*

South Africa is also a comfortable place to visit with good roads and hotels. Much of the land there is privately owned and fenced so you should obtain permission from the owner before entering. Although plenty of books will tell you about good places to look, part of the fun is to search likely places and see what you find. After some practice you get to know what sort of terrain is worth a look, for instance white quartzite areas are often rich in succulents. Even so, plants can be unpredictable and can turn up in unlikely places. Intrepid enthusiasts are still finding new locations for known plants and completely new species. Since so many of the plants from this region are tiny, it is likely that there are more still to find.

For the more adventurous traveller, the country with the greatest concentration of cactus species is Mexico. Here you can find spectacular hillsides covered with forests of huge columnar cacti as well as many of the choicest, most desirable cactus species growing in the wild (see page 115). So there are plenty of reasons to go to this beautiful country, which is why it has been such

a popular destination for cactus enthusiasts for decades, particularly from the USA. Many accounts of expeditions during the early part of the twentieth century are recorded in the Journal of the Cactus and Succulent Society of America. In those days, it was common practice to dig up wild plants, but Mexican law now strictly prohibits the collection of plants and seeds. As a result of this and the increased incidence of crime, expeditions of this kind are less popular nowadays. However, many people still visit Mexico, hire a vehicle, and visit cactus habitats without difficulty, but it is sensible to go in a group, ideally with someone who speaks Spanish and knows the country.

Finally there is South America, famous for its fantastic diversity of cactus habitats. With so many countries to choose from it is difficult to recommend any one in particular, they are all different and each has something to offer the adventurous traveller. Many of the cactus species live in the Andes so are found in Chile, Argentina, Bolivia, Peru and Equador, as well as a few in Columbia and Venezuela.

They look just like saguaros in the Sonoran desert, but these are Echinopsis pasacana *growing in northern Argentina.*

21

OPPOSITE: Quartzite sand patches like this one in Minas Gerais, Brazil are the only places where Uebelmannia gummifera *grows.*

Matucana aurantiaca flowering at high altitude, west of Cajamarca in Peru.

Chile has few genera but the popular genus copiapoa and the majority of eriosyce come from there, mainly living in the north of the country at low altitude near the long sea coast of the Atacama desert. It is a pleasant country to visit with good infrastructure and many comfortable places to stay, mainly on the coast. To visit some of the best cactus habitats it is necessary to use dirt roads of variable quality – they are often sandy, so a four-wheel-drive vehicle is desirable.

The north-west of Argentina is the best part of the country for cactus hunting with a wide range of genera to be seen, and the pleasant city of Salta is a good place to start. On the eastern edge of the Andes, the scenery is spectacular and cacti are extremely plentiful in the dry valleys. Most places can be reached by road and simple hotels may be found in the main towns.

Further north, Peru is the most diverse in terms of habitat types: the dry coastal plain similar to that of northern Chile, dry coastal valleys, high-altitude altiplano and warm, wet valleys in the north-east of the country. While a visit is worthwhile just for the spectacular scenery and remarkable Inca remains such as Machu Picchu, a large number of cactus genera may be found in Peru, most of which are columnar, including some spectacular genera such as espostoa, armatocereus and weberbauerocereus. It is also the home of matucanas with their unusual flowers, and oroya. Many habitats can be visited on good roads even though most are not tarred, but many roads in the mountains are narrow and winding requiring care and a vehicle with high clearance.

Equador only has a few species in the dry valleys of the south and is an extension of what can be found in northern Peru.

Bolivia has many popular globular cacti such as rebutia, echinopsis and parodia, and is mainly high-altitude altiplano with lowland to the east. This hot lowland, known as the Chaco, is difficult to explore because of the dense growth of bushes and inhospitable climate. It extends into Paraguay where a few rarely visited cacti are found. Bolivia has a poorly developed infrastructure and travel can be difficult but the people are hospitable and the prices very reasonable.

The best time to visit Andean habitats is from October to January when most of the cacti will flower and the weather is usually pleasant although with an increasing incidence of rain particularly in the afternoons.

In the east of the continent is Brazil, a huge country with many unique cactus genera, of which most are cereoids. There are a number of different climatic zones, some with interesting cacti, such as the grassland areas of Rio Grande do Sul, which extend into Uruguay, where you can find parodia, frailea and some gymnocalyciums. Further north the climate is more tropical and cacti occur either among the trees in the caatinga, an open forest with a pronounced dry season, or on rock outcrops in the forest that can be difficult to find unless you know where to look. It is the dream of many enthusiasts to

see discocactus, melocactus and the amazing species of uebelmannia in their natural surroundings.

The plants flower for much of the year, so the best time to go is probably from June to August when it is not too hot. Brazil is an inexpensive place to visit with good roads and accommodation. The national language is Portuguese and, like most of South America, few people outside the cities speak any English.

Conservation

All cacti and many other succulents are protected by international and local conservation regulations so it is illegal to collect plants and often seeds from plants in the wild. You may think that it will make no difference just to take one or two but the cumulative effect of many people doing this can have a disastrous impact on a plant population. With improvements in cultural and propagating techniques, most desirable plants are now available to growers from artificially propagated plants in cultivation, so there is no excuse for stealing plants from habitat.

While the wholesale removal of plants by collectors has now been largely stopped, illegal activity continues to occur. Money can still facilitate the removal of plants from private land and their subsequent export to wealthy but unscrupulous collectors. The evidence can sometimes be seen where all the plants of a saleable size have been removed from a population, leaving holes in the ground. Where a species has a very limited distribution, this can cause its extinction. However, this is not the only threat to the plants and for many species other factors have always had much more influence on their survival.

Every year, countless succulents are destroyed by over-grazing, road building, urban expansion, reservoir construction, mining, agriculture, intentional fires, charcoal production, and so on. This is not new, we can only guess at the number of succulents that lived on the grasslands of the USA before the farmers ploughed them up in the early days of colonization. It is fortunate that many species live in places that are of little use to man, such as rocky mountainsides or dry deserts, but even these are not safe forever. Recent irrigation of the dry coastal plain of Peru for agriculture threatens the habitats of some very localized cacti. Similarly, the dry valleys of central Chile have been irrigated in order to expand the country's successful wine industry, which has led to the destruction of all the cacti which grew there. In some countries, South Africa for example, opencast mining of minerals has led to the complete removal of whole mountains, resulting in the loss of all the plants growing there. And so the list goes on – although there are organizations doing conservation work, little impact has been made on the overall picture.

New Discoveries

Ever since plant exploration began, new genera and species of succulents have been discovered and described. Many of the early descriptions were imprecise and leave doubt as to what plant they referred to. There are many articles in the specialist literature about tracking down which plants known today were being described then. It often comes down to an educated guess as to their identity and an increasing trend is to dismiss these names and replace them with a more recent one that can be unambiguously assigned to a known plant (see page 13).

As previously mentioned, much of the work of exploration and documentation was done by horticulturalists and enthusiastic amateurs rather than trained botanists. One result of this was that many 'new' species were, in fact, no more than local forms of plants already described. This continues to a

Ariocarpus like these were once imported legally from Mexico in large quantities, but now it is forbidden.

lesser extent today with many new descriptions appearing every year, not all of which are truly worthy of recognition. These are published in any of a number of specialist succulent titles and general botanical publications. To help keep track of all these, the IOS publishes *Repertorium Plantarum Succulentarum*, an annual listing of all the new taxa for the year, which provides a useful reference to the origin of names. A very useful compendium of all the names for cacti from 1950 to 1990 has been published as a single volume *The IOS Index of Names of Cactaceae* and a similar one for other succulents for the period 1950 to 1992 is also available. Both reference works will tell you whether the name is validly published and where to find the original publication.

There are still novelties being discovered and described like this Yavia cryptocarpa from northern Argentina, which was only given a name in 2001.

Field Numbers

Some plant hunters have visited succulent habitats and allocated numbers to the plant populations they found. These usually take the form of letters followed by a number, for example SB352 refers to an echinocereus found by Steven Brack. There are no standards for this activity so it has not been done consistently; some numbers refer to individual populations whilst others may be re-used when similar plants are seen at other localities. These numbers often follow the plant name in seed or plant catalogues.

Propagating plants of known origin is a valuable conservation activity since it reduces the need to re-collect the plant from the wild. The problem is that if you see plants in cultivation bearing such numbers, there is usually no way of determining how many generations separate the individuals from the original collection of seed or plants. To address this issue, the Chileans, a society for the study of South American cacti , has published a code to help establish authenticity in cultivated plants. The field number is followed by a letter in parentheses with the following meaning:

(H) = cutting of habitat plant
(Z) = grown from seed out of a fruit produced by pollination in habitat
(Y) = grown from seed collected from the pollination of habitat plants in cultivation

This convention has been adopted by a number of amateur propagators as well as a few nurserymen, and it is to be hoped that wider acceptance will follow. The increasing regulation of plants and seed collected from the wild leads to an inevitable reduction in new genetic material being introduced into cultivated stock. There is a danger that most plants in cultivation will derive from a few individuals that are maintained in seed-producing nurseries, leading to a loss of the rich diversity within each species. Even worse would be the proliferation of unintentional hybrids, eventually resulting in the pure species becoming lost. The careful propagation of authentic material is a useful activity every amateur can undertake to reduce the pressure on wild populations.

3 Cultivation, Propagation and Display

Gardening as a pastime continues to increase in popularity as our leisure time becomes more important to us. Garden centres have never done better business as the peace and quiet of our gardens become ever more valuable in our hectic lives. Everyone needs a relaxing contrast to the stresses of earning a living – something that moves slowly, is undemanding, yet fulfilling. The cultivation of plants has brought satisfaction to millions and today it is probably the most popular hobby of all. For most, the tending of a small plot of land around the house, raising a few annuals from seed or tending hanging baskets and patio pots is enough. But for some, plants hold a fascination and they need to delve a bit deeper and perhaps specialize in a particular kind of plant. It was probably in childhood that most of us bought our first cactus or two that we kept on a window-ledge. For some it was a passing interest, a fleeting fascination, but to others it was the start of a lifelong interest that would re-

A specialist collection of just one genus, in this case the small-growing conophytum.

The British Cactus and Succulent Society promotes its activities at large horticultural shows.

emerge in later life to become a multi-faceted hobby. So what is it that makes it appeal to so many people? For some, it is the satisfaction of growing something for many years, eventually to be rewarded by exquisite blooms. For others, it is the thrill of competition at shows or the companionship of like-minded friends from whom there is always something to learn. But why succulents? Well, they are in many ways the ultimate plant, the extreme adaptation to a hostile environment, sometimes perfectly symmetrical and other times strange, even grotesque.

As well as actually cultivating cacti and succulents, there are many other aspects to the hobby. You can take photographs of the plants both in cultivation and in their exotic habitats; there is plenty of scope for artistry particularly in close-up images of their intricate details. There is much to know about their ecology, such as their varied pollination mechanisms, some of which are amongst the most complicated in the plant world. They give you a reason to travel to the most dramatic places but perhaps the best part of all is the opportunity to make friends around the world. Enthusiasts are usually amiable people and it is often the case that an introduction through the hobby leads to the discovery of other common interests, for instance, succulent growers have often been tropical fish keepers at some time in their lives. Another associated activity is stamp collecting, and the two are sometimes combined by those who collect the many issues featuring succulent plants in their designs. Although some of the best stamps have been issued by countries with succulents among their native flora, many have been featured by countries where they are just cultivated as a hobby.

The best way to meet like-minded people is to join a local group. The British Cactus and Succulent Society (BCSS) has approximately 100 branches all around the UK. The meetings are usually held monthly and at each one there will be some entertainment: usually a speaker, sometimes a discussion or perhaps a quiz. Many branches have a monthly table competition, which is an ideal place for beginners to learn about competitive showing. Some branches organize an annual show, and groups of branches, known as 'zones', put on more ambitious events such as conventions with overseas speakers or larger shows.

Most beginners buy any plant they like the look of and soon find their glasshouse is full, particularly if they have some of the fast-growing species. Many collectors will eventually dispose of the easily grown, 'common' plants in favour of the choicer, slower-growing or difficult species that present more of a challenge to cultivate and do better at shows. Others will decide to specialize in a single genus or a number of genera, whilst usually retaining a few favourites of diverse affinity. There is a human desire to 'collect the set' and this is fairly easy with some genera but if you choose, for instance, euphor-

Cacti and succulents can form the basis of a thematic collection of postage stamps. These are Peruvian stamps, issued to promote conservation.

bia then you have little chance. A complete collection of mammillaria would also take a lot of glasshouse space but big genera like these are the most popular specialities. The problem with specializing is that you tend to look for smaller and smaller differences and miss out on the diversity of succulents in general.

To cater for the specialist, there are many small societies and study groups, most of which have an international membership. These groups can provide a wealth of in-depth information and some offer seeds or plants that would be difficult to find elsewhere. Membership also includes the benefit of receiving their regular publications which, as well as providing information, contain useful advertisements for plants, seeds, sundries and books. Back issues are usually available, which are particularly valuable, as much of the information cannot be found in books on the subject.

Collecting plants is not like collecting antiques or toy cars – you always have the opportunity to make more of what you have by propagation and in so doing you help protect the plants in the wild from illegal collecting. Even if you only have one individual of a species, you can propagate it by cuttings or grafting. If you have at least two plants of the same species then you have a chance to cross-pollinate them, produce seed and raise many individuals. The scope and quality of your plant collection is not simply down to how much money you have available to spend, rather it is very much dependent on your skill as a cultivator, since even the rarest plant can be grown from relatively inexpensive seed if you know how to do it. Similarly, if you buy a rare and expensive plant, it will not thrive and grace your collection for long unless you look after it properly. A plant-growing hobby is very satisfying – testimony to every year you have spent cultivating them, slowly getting bigger and more impressive, even if they only fill a small pot after thirty years!

Ornamental Planting

Many succulents are suitable for temporary placement outdoors in northern Europe and places with a similar climate. Even in a single summer, the spination of some cacti can get noticeably stronger as a result of not growing under glass, perhaps because of the greater

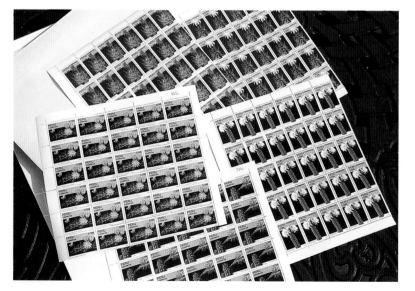

Southern Europe has many spectacular outdoor collections like this garden in Barcelona, the Costa y Lobera.

The famous Jardin Exotique, which stands on a steep cliff-side overlooking Monaco.

BELOW: The cactus garden at Guatiza, Lanzarote is one of many on the Canary Islands. Photo: Eddie Cheetham

intensity of ultraviolet light. Many species can be left outside for all the year and so long as excess moisture can be avoided the list is quite extensive. Some species of opuntia, escobaria, echinocereus and a few of the choice North American cacti can survive cold but will not tolerate water logging. Many yuccas and agaves are also reliably hardy in the UK and thrive in a sunny position where the soil drains away water quickly. If you want to try creating a rockery for succulents, you need to build the level up with well-drained soil against a sunny wall. Ideally, build a removable roof over the top to keep the rain off during the winter and this will improve the chances of success.

Where the climate is suitable – sunny and reasonably dry in summer, mild in winter with little or short-lived frosts – cacti and succulents may be used to make permanent outdoor displays. Many of the best displays may be found in parks and gardens around the Mediterranean, on the Canary Islands, in South Africa and in the southwest of the USA. Visiting these gardens gives an impression of the dimensions that succulents

Large aloes dominate this view of the Karoo Gardens. Photo: Daphne Pritchard

The Karoo Botanic Gardens in Worcester, South Africa is famous for its landscape planting of succulents. Photo: Eddie Harris

can achieve in the wild, although they are usually planted much closer together than they would grow in habitat. The plants on display are generally the larger growing species, which most of us are unable to grow to maturity in our glasshouses. Fruits of species for which seed collection in habitat is no longer possible are produced in many of these outdoor collections and indeed this is now an important source for commercial cactus production.

Places to see Succulents in Outdoor Plantings

USA
Arizona: Sonora Desert Botanical Garden, Tucson; Desert Botanical Garden, Phoenix.
California: Huntington Botanical Gardens, Los Angeles; Lotusland, Los Angeles; Rancho Santa Ana Botanic Garden, Claremont; University of California Botanical Garden, Berkeley.

Canary Islands
Desierto Feliz, Tenerife; Jardin Canario, Gran Canaria; Jardin de Cactus, Lanzarote.

France
Les Cedres, St Jean-Cap Ferrat, Alpes Maritimes.

Italy
Hanbury Gardens, La Mortola, Ventimiglia.

Monaco
Jardin Exotique de Monaco, Monte Carlo.

Spain
Costa y Lobera, Barcelona; Pinya da Rosa, Blanes; Botanicactus, Ses Salinas, Mallorca.

South Africa
Karoo National Botanic Garden, Worcester, Cape Province; National Botanic Garden, Kirstenbosch, Cape Province; Pretoria Botanic Garden, Pretoria, Transvaal.

Shows

For some growers, participation in competitive shows provides a major incentive to further improve the quality of their plants. Although cactus and succulent growing is popular all over

the world, the concept of competing against other growers to win prizes is not universal. Only in Britain and the USA is it an established part of the calendar, although societies in other countries have recently begun to introduce shows as regular events. The history of showing goes back a long way and reports of competitions can be found in journals dating from the

Succulents can be used outdoors in summer in the UK to make an attractive display.

The plantings at the Desert Botanical Garden in Phoenix, Arizona, are impressively mature.

31

Lotusland in Los Angeles is a spectacular garden of succulents and other exotic plants.

Huntington Gardens near Los Angeles has a well-established collection of succulents in its extensive grounds.

members selling plants, seeds or books at very reasonable prices. These amateur propagators regularly offer species that are difficult to find in the trade. Shows are also ideal places to meet people who will give you advice and encouragement plus the chance to see species you may have only seen in pictures. This is particularly true of regional and national shows where the very best examples of the cultivators' skills are on display.

To maintain consistency across the UK, the BCSS has for many years maintained guidelines for its shows. These have become the accepted standards and are published in a regularly updated booklet entitled *The Handbook of Shows*, which contains everything you need to know if you want to take part in, or even organize a show.

A commercial display by Southfield Nurseries at a show in the UK demonstrates what can be achieved with expert culture.

end of the nineteenth century. The idea is to reward the skill of the cultivator, skills that will need to have been applied over a much longer period than that needed for success with many other types of plant. It is one of the rewards of growing these plants that every year's investment is there to be seen, unlike annual crops where you must start from the beginning every year. It can be disheartening as a beginner to see the prizes awarded to plants that have been in cultivation for decades, but then there are always classes where young plants can compete, such as those with pot size restrictions. Most shows also have special classes for novices and juniors as a step towards the main classes.

Shows are usually the main event of the year, great social gatherings where members can meet and see each other's best plants. There are often

A critical aspect of any show is the quality of the judging. The BCSS runs an annual course, comprising a series of lectures, for members wishing to become approved judges. They will already need to have experience of cultivating and recognizing a wide range of cacti and succulents in order to be able to evaluate one exhibit against another. Even qualified judges have to attend every few years to keep their knowledge of new plants and changes in the Handbook up to date. On the last day of the course the participants have to judge a mock show and their performance is assessed to see whether they achieve the standard necessary to judge BCSS shows. Each class in a show is open to exhibits that meet certain stated criteria, such as botanical relationship, number of plants, and

Visitors enjoy the exhibits at a national show held by the British Cactus and Succulent Society.

Attractive glazed containers and artistically grown plants characterize shows in the USA.

pot size. The Handbook defines suitable groupings of related plants that make a good basis for show classes, so judges need to know if the plants they see before them are admissible in the class they are entered. It should be said that to become a judge is only possible after years of experience and there are currently fewer than 100 in the UK, but it is something to aspire to.

Entering shows is something everyone should do as part of the hobby. The criteria used to judge one exhibit against another are explained in the Handbook and are designed to encourage and reward good cultivation. Points are awarded for each exhibit out of a possible maximum of twenty, allocated as follows:

General appearance	5
Maturity (age)	5
Evidence of flowering	2
Freedom from pests and diseases	2
Difficulty of cultivation	3
Rarity (in cultivation)	1
Presentation	2

From this it can be seen that plants which are well grown and of greatest age are the most likely to win, particularly if they are difficult to grow. Presentation refers to such things as the correctness of the planting, cleanliness of the pot and neatness of the label. In the USA, judging of exhibits is based on similar criteria but the presentation tends to be given greater emphasis. It is apparent in American shows that exhibitors

take more trouble over choosing containers and the artistic placement of the plant in them. The use of ceramic pots rather than plastic ones is widespread as is the inclusion of rocks for artistic effect. Succulent bonsai, where plants are trained into windswept shapes, can add spectacle to a display and are very popular in the USA.

The largest and most important show in the UK is the BCSS National Show, which is held every four years. The next show will be in August 2004 at Spalding, Lincolnshire. Details of this and all future events may be found on the BCSS website.

Hybrids, Cristates and Variegated Plants

Hybrids

Most cacti and succulents in cultivation are species, collectors historically preferring to grow a plant that is not a hybrid. Care is taken by seed producers not to produce hybrids by accident although in some genera it is difficult to prevent since species are often able to cross-pollinate. However, for the commercial nursery producing plants for the general market, the short flowering period of most species is a major limitation, and hybridization offers the possibility of growing plants with better flowers which are produced over a longer period.

The cacti that have been the subject of hybridization for the longest time are the epi-

A 'Jewel' hybrid of Mammillaria carmenae raised by Southfield Nurseries, UK.

BELOW: *Rebutia hybrid 'Celebration' bred for colour and long flowering by Southfield Nurseries, UK.*

phyllums, the so-called 'orchid cacti'. These epiphytic cacti are well suited to being grown indoors and make good houseplants. The large flowers come in a range of colours and are freely produced from the flat leaf-like stems. They are easy to propagate from stem cuttings and present no difficulties in cultivation so long as they are grown in acidic compost rich in humus.

Astrophytums have also been hybridized, all the species have been used but the most popular are hybrids involving A. asterias as a parent. Much of the development has been done in Japan and the remarkable strain known as 'Super Kabuto' with spectacular markings is now commonly seen in collections.

Echinopsis has been extensively hybridized to perfect the flowers and extend the flowering period. In the USA, the Paramount hybrids of Harry Johnson have remained popular and more recently the Schick hybrids distributed by International Succulent Introductions have revitalized interest in this aspect of the hobby. Hybridization continues between echinopsis and other related genera with the objective of producing plants with bigger or more attractive flowers, ideally blooming regularly throughout the growing season.

In England, Abbey Brook Nursery has been working on these for many years and has distributed a number of attractive named hybrids. Southfield Nursery has produced a number of hybrids of rebutia that maintain the free-flowering properties of the species in an extended range of colours with a greater amount of repeat flowering. These make good plants for a sunny window-sill since they can tolerate some shade and the spines are relatively soft and harmless.

Succulents have also been the subjects of extensive hybridization. Aloes, for example, hybridize readily, even with species from other genera such as gasteria. Another popular houseplant, *Euphorbia millii*, the 'crown of thorns', has been used as a parent for a number of successful hybrids. Adenium hybrids are popular in warm climates for their large swollen stems and spectacular flowers, which are freely produced for much of the year. Echeverias, once more popular than they are today, hybridize easily and these are more often seen than the species they were bred from.

Echeveria hybrid 'Galaxy' selected for its neat rosettes and pretty flowers.

Echeveria hybrid 'Ebony', one of many popular hybrids of this genus.

Natural hybrids of cacti and other succulents can sometimes be found in the wild: usually just isolated individuals are discovered amongst large numbers of the parents. The hybrids are often sterile, so unable to set seed and produce further generations. They usually have features that are intermediate between the parents, but it is not always obvious what the parents were since a small species may have crossed with a very large one and the resulting hybrid might look very different from both. Situations like this have led to botanical names being applied to these hybrids as if they were species.

An example of the large-flowered hybrids of Euphorbia milli *that make such good houseplants.*

Cristates

A cristate plant is one where the growing point has become a growing line so that the resulting plant has the shape of a ribbon, rather than a sphere or a cylinder, as would be the case for most cacti. Cristates are found in a diverse assortment of succulents, as they are in many non-succulent plants. The reason for a plant to adopt this curious form of growth has been the subject of speculation ever since it was first observed but no explanation has gained universal acceptance. Anyone who grows a lot of plants from seed will have noticed that an occasional seedling will be obviously cristate soon after germination. It can occur in just about any genus but some species appear to be more prone to it than others, and for these there can be a number of cristate forms of the same species that differ in appearance.

The linear nature of the growth of a young cristate plant eventually causes it to push down on the soil near each end of the growing line, so tending to lift the roots out of the soil. If the ribbon of growth is thin, it is able to curl, so relieving the pressure and allowing the plant to thrive on its own roots. However, in species such as *Echinocactus grusonii*, the ribbon is too wide to curl and the fan-like growth pushes the plant upwards. Cristates are often grafted for propagation but for these wide forms, they have to be grafted on a tall stock for survival.

On occasions, a plant that has been quite normal for many years will suddenly start to grow cristate or perhaps one of the heads in a clump will start to grow cristate. Conversely,

Cristate heads can appear in a normal clump as you can see on this Copiapoa dealbata *in Chile.*

The most natural cristates are those that occur spontaneously like this Mammillaria pectinifera.

If you grow enough seedlings, you are likely to get a few cristates like this Mammillaria zeilmanniana.

cristate plants often start to grow normal heads, a phenomenon known as reversion. If not removed, these reversions will tend to take over like suckers do with a rose bush, so they should be cut off when small to avoid leaving too much of a scar. In old plants, the growing line can become extremely long, although this is not always obvious because of its contorted shape. Perhaps it is because of the potential for so much growth from this line that cristates tend to grow bigger than their normal counterparts.

The occasional cristate can be found amongst plant populations in the wild and in some places a significant proportion of the plants are cristates. This may have been caused by some infection that spread among the plants, or

Cristates usually bloom with normal flowers like this rebutia, but sometimes even the flowers are cristate.

perhaps an inherited propensity to form cristates. Although you can buy seed from a cristate parent, there does not appear to be any evidence to suggest that the seedlings are more likely to be cristates themselves. There are collectors who specialize in these plants and it is interesting to see a group together and try to guess what species they are since their appearance is often very different from the normal form.

Another aberrant form of succulent where there are many growing points in place of the usual one is known as monstrose. This is less common and rather more curious than attractive, but monstrose cerei are often seen and can be raised from seed.

Variegated Plants

Many of the popular garden plants offered for sale are variegated forms and are valuable because of the bright colours of those parts of the plant that are usually green. The leaves often have patches of yellow or red due to the absence of chlorophyll that usually masks these other colours. Similarly, the green stems or

Occasionally, a seedling can exhibit patches of variegation like this Echinopsis leucantha.

This variegated form of euphorbia grows quickly and is popular for indoor landscaping.

These variegated cacti are grafted onto hylocereus to keep them alive, but they must be kept warm. People often think the coloured part is a flower!

Variegated haworthias like this H. fasciata *are much prized by specialist collectors.*

leaves of succulents occasionally produce variegated forms that can sometimes be perpetuated by propagation but are often unstable.

The most commonly seen variegated cactus is the red form of *Gymnocalycium mihanovichi*, known as 'Ruby Ball' (*see* illustration bottom right). It is a bright orange-red and so lacking in chlorophyll that it can only survive when grafted on to a green stock capable of photosynthesis. In recent years, various other colour forms of this plant have been selected and propagated as well as brightly coloured forms of other species such as *Echinopsis chamaecereus* becoming available. The best colour is maintained by keeping the plants in light shade.

Most of these plants are commercially produced in the Far East and grafted on to hylocereus, a triangular-stemmed species that is sensitive to cold and should be kept above 10°C (50°F) in winter. For permanent culture it would be a good idea to re-graft it on to a more robust stock.

Location (Temperature and Light)

To grow the best quality succulents, location is the first and probably the most important consideration. Generally speaking, the warmer the climate, the easier it is to provide the conditions that plants will enjoy. However, most succulents have evolved in climates with seasons characterized by periods of drought or cold, possibly both. Even those that inhabit the tropics often live at high altitude where the climate is cooler and subject to diurnal temperature variations which the plants need to grow.

For most of us the challenge is to make sure that the plants are sufficiently warm and receiving enough sunshine. However, if you live in a tropical lowland area where the weather is always hot and humid, then the succulents you can grow well will be limited to the relatively few species that naturally live in places with such a climate. As far as cacti are concerned,

Cacti benefit from being put outside in summer, particularly when the weather is warm like here in southern Germany.

the tropical species from Brazil and the Caribbean would be the best choices, melocactus being the obvious example. With succulents, there are many from tropical Africa that would do well, such as some euphorbias and various caudiciform succulents. (Caudiciform is a term used to describe plants from many families that survive periods of drought by storing water in a swollen, perennial storage organ known as a caudex.)

In Europe, the ideal climate may be found around the Mediterranean. In southern Spain, southern France and Italy, many species thrive outdoors and spectacular outdoor plantings have been established (see page 31). A similar climate can be found in parts of Australia and the south-west of the USA where California has become a centre of commercial cactus growing because of its near-ideal environment. Here, the reliably sunny days and cool nights enable a vast range of species to be grown so long as each is given an appropriate level of protection from rainfall and sunshine. If you live in a less favourable area with a short growing season, the results obtained by skilled growers with these idyllic conditions may seem quite astonishing. Perhaps you can console yourself with the thought that the challenge you face adds to the pleasure of success!

Succulent growing is very popular in the countries of northern Europe. A glasshouse is essential for the serious hobbyist, however a

If you live in southern California, then the larger cacti can be grown outside with ease.

smaller collection can be housed in a conservatory or even on a sunny window-ledge but eventually the plants outgrow their surroundings and a glasshouse becomes the only answer.

There is a long history of the hobby in eastern Europe where the winters are extremely cold and heating a glasshouse is too expensive, even for those that are partly underground, a design that was once popular in cold climates. In such circumstances, once the plants are dry and have stopped growing for the winter, they can be brought into the house and many species will survive indoors, away from bright light, until the spring, when they can be returned to the glasshouse.

Fortunately, for those Europeans who live further west, the winters are generally less severe and the plants may be left in a glasshouse all the year round so long as there is adequate heating.

The siting of the glasshouse is very important, but there may not be much choice if your garden is fairly small. Rooftop glasshouses are popular in places where a property has insufficient land and where they are permitted by planning laws. They usually have the advantage of an unobstructed view of the sun and can even be incorporated into the heating system of the house.

The glasshouse should be situated in the sunniest place possible, avoiding shade from trees or buildings. If you have the option of orientating your glasshouse in any direction, it is generally considered best to have the ridge run in

The larger aloes are popular subjects in garden landscapes in the south west of the USA.

The modern cultivation of cacti in glasshouses was pioneered in the Netherlands and Belgium.

a north-south direction to maximize the sun's energy passing through the glass; lean-tos are best on a south-facing wall in the northern hemisphere.

Winter sun is particularly valuable, so bear in mind that when the sun is lower in the sky obstructions will be more of a consideration. This advice is based on the principal that you can always shade plants in a sunny glasshouse but you cannot make a shaded glasshouse sunny. Sun is not only important for the strong growth of spines but it encourages flowering and generally heats the glasshouse, so allowing

The environment of a large glasshouse like this one at Kew is computer controlled.

Potted plants standing on metal trays, surrounded by white-painted wooden sides.

you to ventilate more whilst maintaining the temperature. A common problem in cultivation is lack of light and this is often seen with plants grown in a house, the new growth gets drawn up and is unhealthily thin, a condition known as etiolation.

There are many different types of glasshouse available and the one you choose will depend on cost, aesthetics, size and proposed use. When deciding on the size, it is worth bearing in mind that experience suggests it will soon not be big enough. It is probably best to buy the largest you can afford that will fit in your garden. Larger glasshouses, being less prone to temperature changes, are better for the plants, and the greater volume of contained air helps to improve ventilation and reduce the risk of scorching.

The cheapest structures are polythene tunnels, which have improved technologically over recent years, and are very good for growing succulents so long as you choose the right covering. The light transmission and thermal properties make them a popular choice for commercial growers but they are not very attractive in a garden setting and have to re-covered periodically.

The most popular glasshouse designs are those constructed from aluminium, which have the advantages of low maintenance and better light transmission than wooden ones since they have narrower glazing bars. Aluminium is not as warm as wood and can be more difficult to line with polythene if you choose to use it to improve insulation in winter, but they are still most people's choice. Cheaply constructed models are prone to damage by high winds so should not be erected in exposed situations, and in all cases, the frame should be securely fixed to heavy foundations. Double-walled plastic sheeting is sometimes used to glaze the frame and this is good for both light transmission and insulation. However, the resulting structure is not as rigid as glass so the frame may need to be stronger to be suitable for this kind of 'glazing'. Whichever type of glasshouse you choose, make sure that you specify the maximum number and size of ventilators possible.

Humidity can be a problem in a succulent glasshouse, particularly if insufficient ventilation is provided in winter (see page 43). To prevent dampness rising from the floor, a few inches of hardcore should be spread over the earth, compacted and then covered with a thick polythene liner. At least 5cm (2in) of concrete or paving slabs over this will provide a dry floor on which to walk, stand pots and place staging supports. Getting this level will facilitate the construction of level staging on which to stand the plants.

You can grow plants on the floor of your glasshouse or tunnel, but for most people the use of benching is preferred since it makes the routine maintenance easier and brings plants up to a level where they can be studied and enjoyed. The aluminium staging supplied for glasshouses is expensive and can be insufficiently strong for a collection of succulents because of the heavy nature of the soil and the proximity of the pots. An easy way to make your own strong benching is to buy second-hand steel shelving angle (such as Dexion) and make a well-braced framework from that. The environment will be dry enough to prevent it rusting to any great extent, particularly if you paint it first, and it has the advantage of being stronger than the aluminium version.

The top of the benching can be made from various materials, some growers favouring an open galvanized steel mesh that lets water drain quickly and allows air to circulate among the pots. It also reduces the risk of pests spreading from one pot to another and is well suited to species that are sensitive to stagnant moisture such as stapeliads. However, for most species,

this construction will demand more frequent watering and there is a risk that some pots are never properly wetted, particularly in spring after the long, dry winter rest. A good solution is to cover the frame with strong boards such as cement fibre sheets to provide support on which trays can be placed.

These shallow trays can be the standard horticultural plastic type or made from thin sheets of aluminium such as used offset printing plates, a waste product of the printing industry. These can be cut to size, scored about 2cm (0.75in) in from the edge and folded to make a tray; the corners can be easily sealed with bathroom sealant. Being able to construct trays of exactly the right size makes best use of the space available and is ideal for shelves. The edges of the benches can be fitted with painted wooden boards which, as well as looking neat, protect the pots from direct sunlight and accidental damage.

The trays can be watertight or provided with a drainage hole. Watertight trays have the advantage of facilitating watering from below so long as they are level. It takes a little practice to know how much water to give each tray, but this approach is the best way to ensure the whole pot of soil is wetted, particularly if it has completely dried out. It was once a common practice to put a layer of gravel in the trays, but this adds to the weight and increases the risk of pest infestation. Keeping your glasshouse clean is a vital activity in the war against pests and it is much easier to clean and disinfect an empty tray than one with gravel in it.

Square pots look very neat when used for a collection of haworthias.

matter of judgement as to how many shelves to construct and where to put them to avoid creating too much shade.

Heating

A major consideration for any glasshouse is the choice of heating method. There are appliances utilizing electricity, gas, paraffin or fuel oil that are suitable for use in a glasshouse; the decision on which to choose depends on a number of factors including glasshouse size, locality, fuel availability and minimum temperature desired.

Once very popular because of its modest price, paraffin has the disadvantages of needing regular attention, a lack of control and the risk of the heater producing damaging smoke if not properly maintained. Natural gas can be economic if already available on site, but a freestanding heater will generate humidity, making ventilation essential. If any fuel-burning heater is not vented outside the glasshouse then it will create water as a by-product, which will increase humidity, a consideration that makes this kind of heating less suitable for succulents.

For smaller glasshouses, the best choice is an electric fan heater placed on the floor, since it is dry and easily controlled. Where cheap electricity is available during the night, this can significantly reduce the running costs. The fan, which should be left running continuously, helps to combat layering of the air, so preventing warm air remaining in the roof and cold air accumulating near the floor. The extra ventilation and dry air also reduces the risk from fungal infections, a major cause of plant death in winter. The usual choice for large glasshouses are space heaters powered by fuel oil or gas that have external flues to remove the combustion products and powerful fans to distribute the warm air. These are excellent in all respects although their initial purchase and installation is expensive.

It is a common practice for growers to line the inside of their glasshouse with a transparent polythene sheet or 'bubble' in the winter. This is a time-consuming and difficult job but significantly reduces the heating bill. It can also prevent drips from leaks or condensation reaching the plants, but the disadvantages are the reduction in light and the potential loss of ventilation that usually comes from gaps in the glasshouse construction. If you do line with

Glasshouses in cold climates are often lined with polythene in winter.

As your collection grows due to new acquisitions and successful cultivation, then the temptation to erect shelves can be irresistible. If you place sun-loving plants on these shelves, being near to the glass, they will probably thrive and indeed some species will only flower reliably if they are given such conditions. The problem is that plants beneath the shelves will receive less light and this can be detrimental to their development. Shelves in a glasshouse can be a benefit but too often it results in some plants suffering from lack of light, so it is a polythene in winter, do not be tempted to leave it up all the year since the loss of light is detrimental to many species, and avoid using old pieces year after year since they become ever more opaque.

The minimum temperature you decide to maintain depends on which species you want to grow. Most collectors keep the temperature above 5°C (41°F), which is sufficient for most cacti and many succulents. Small-growing species that need a higher temperature such as some Madagascan succulents, or cacti such as discocactus and melocactus can be accommodated in a propagator within the glasshouse that can easily be kept at a higher temperature. It actually doesn't cost any more since any escaping heat contributes to the overall heating, and a cabinet with glass or plastic panels and a thermostatically controlled tubular heater with a fan to circulate the air can easily be constructed. In summer, the panels can be removed to increase the light intensity reaching the plants. Of course, if you want to grow large plants of tender species like some pachypodiums, alluadias, and Brazilian columnar cacti such as pilosocereus, arrojadoa and micranthocereus, then you will need to heat the whole glasshouse to at least 10°C (50°F). Generally speaking, every increase of 5°C (41°F) in the minimum temperature doubles the cost, which may account for the fact that large specimens of these tender species are not common in collections.

Ventilation

Just as important as heating, ventilation is often neglected by succulent enthusiasts. In habitat, plants are used to moving air, and stagnant air can be damaging even to the most arid-adapted species, particularly if it is hot. If you use a fan heater in winter then leave the fan on at all times, even when the heating elements are off. It can be beneficial to leave the fan on in summer, although better still is to have a large fan that turns on when the temperature rises above 20–25°C (68–77°F). In propagators and heated cabinets, the small fans recycled from discarded computers are ideal to keep the air moving, particularly when used in conjunction with electric tubular heaters.

The use of the glasshouse ventilators is also a vital consideration. Most growers fit automatic controllers to their ventilators that open them proportionally to the internal temperature. These are a great benefit and remove the risk of forgetting to open the vents on a warm, sunny day, which could result in scorching of the plants. The only problem is that they close the windows during cool summer nights to maintain the temperature when, in fact, the plants would grow better if the temperature was allowed to drop. Diurnal variation in temperature is beneficial to most succulents since it is what they experience in habitat and what they have evolved to exploit (see page 8). So, if the night temperature is forecast to remain above 10°C (50°F), then the ventilators should be left open since growth of CAM plants will be adversely affected if the internal temperature stays above 20°C (68°F).

Scorching, which in effect is the burning of the epidermis, will scar plants for years or even cause death. It is caused by sunburn and is most likely to happen on a sunny day in early spring when the plants are still soft from the long winter rest. Small glasshouses are more prone to this problem than larger ones where the greater volume appears to facilitate air movement. Plants situated near to the glass and in stagnant air are most likely to be affected, so the solution is to have a fan running and the windows open. Alternatively, the risk can be reduced by painting a light temporary shade on the outside of the glass using one of the products sold for this purpose. Rain will gradually wash it away during the summer, but once plants are in active growth, it can be wiped off to maximize light intensity during the growing season.

Soils

Successful cultivation can only be achieved through the effective combination of all the factors involved and there is no simple foolproof formula. If you get the basics right, you will be able to grow the plants and gain the experience that will enable you to improve your technique.

There are many and varied soil mixtures but so long as other factors such as locality and watering are appropriate then plants will thrive. Succulent growers are always willing to share their expertise including the soil mixes they use. Although the soils seem quite different at first, there are many common features. Considering the diversity of habitats where succulents occur, it is remarkable that most will grow in the same basic mixture, although slight modifications are recommended for certain groups of plants. The most important considerations are texture, pH and nutrients.

In nature, most succulents grow in largely mineral soils formed from weathered rock and containing little humus, but they can often be high in nutrients. Some growers use a similar substrate in cultivation consisting of a mixture of gravel, course sand, crushed lava or other mineral materials, whilst avoiding fine particles that could clog. When using this sort of medium, watering and feeding becomes very important with little margin for error with regard to nutrients and pH – in effect it is like hydroponics. The benefit of this approach is that the texture of the medium remains consistent over time and so the need to re-pot only becomes necessary when the plant outgrows its container. Some plants, such as Chilean cacti, can do particularly well under this regime but many others do not flourish, so until you get experience with soils that are easier to manage, this kind of substrate is not recommended.

So-called soil-less composts have been very popular in recent times. They are manufactured from peat or peat substitutes such as ground bark or coir (coconut fibre) mixed with lime and a fertilizer. These composts can be used for the cultivation of succulents, and in fact are extensively used by commercial growers who usually have special formulations made up which also contain grit, less or no lime, and perhaps a slow-release fertilizer. For the amateur, these composts have a number of disadvantages, the main one being their short life. As the humus ages, it disintegrates and the open texture breaks down so that the small particles pack together resulting in root loss and, once dry, it can be very difficult to re-wet. Another difficulty is that plants in this type of compost need to be constantly fed since fertilizer is quickly washed out. So, although growth can be very good when plants are first put in these soils, their long-term maintenance is problematic. They can, however, be useful for raising seedlings when the ericaceous (lime-free) formula is probably the best.

Soil Mixes

The usual ingredients of soil preparations are loam with peat or substitutes, to which is added grit, course sand or soil conditioners like vermiculite or perlite. Available in bags from a garden centre or DIY shop, they can be of variable quality and manufacturers often fail to supply a consistent product from year to year. Using these ingredients, the following soil mixes will give you a good start to growing plants, after which you can make appropriate modifications in the light of your own experience and circumstances.

- Loam is sterilized topsoil that has been sieved to remove stones. It should be rich in organic matter and free draining with good structure. John Innes (JI) 3 compost can be substituted but only if it contains the correct proportion of loam. Many commercially produced JI composts have too high a proportion of peat; so bagged sterilized loam is recommended.

- Peat or substitutes are useful for opening up the soil and providing air pockets. They do not contain any significant quantity of nutrients, but peat in particular is useful for lowering the pH of the soil. Fibrous peats are best for succulents, since these keep their structure for the longest time. Because of the environmental considerations of peat extraction, various alternatives are being offered to gardeners. Some growers have tried coir but results have been mixed, probably due to the inconsistency of the product. A better alternative seems to be peat-free compost made from ground bark, which has the advantage of retaining its structure for longer than peat, but is less acidic.

- Grit is a key part of any succulent compost since it helps to maintain sharp drainage. It should be sharp (not round) with an ideal size of up to 5mm (0.2in) but with particles less than 1mm sieved out to prevent clogging. It is also important that it be alkaline free, so materials like acid-washed quartzite or flint are commonly used. To reduce weight, some of the grit can be replaced with perlite or horticultural grade vermiculite, both of which absorb water and release it slowly for the plant to use.

The following composts are recommended for the plants listed. Minor modifications can then be made to accommodate plants with specific requirements, such as extra grit for those that are particularly sensitive to moisture. Ingredients should be just moist when mixed.

- Standard mix for the majority of cacti and other succulents

  1 part by volume of sterilized loam (or JI3)
  1 part by volume of peat or a substitute
  1 part by volume of grit

A complete fertilizer including trace elements, added as recommended by the manufacturer

- Mexican mix for astrophytum, coryphantha, echinocactus, ferocactus, mammillaria, stenocactus, thelocactus and 'Mexican Treasures' (see page 115)

  2 parts by volume of sterilized loam (or JI3)
  1 part by volume of peat or a substitute
  2 parts by volume of grit

A complete fertilizer including trace elements, added as recommended by the manufacturer

- Epiphytic mix for epiphytic cacti

  1 part by volume of sterilized loam (or JI3)
  2 parts by volume of peat or a substitute
  1 part by volume of grit (part of which can be replaced with perlite or vermiculite for weight saving)

A complete fertilizer including trace elements, added as recommended by the manufacturer

pH is Critical

This is a measure of the acidity or alkalinity of a compost. Many species are extremely sensitive to this and if the pH is too high (alkaline) or too low (acid) then growth will be reduced or completely stopped. It is very important to get the pH of the soil right when it is mixed, then it needs to be maintained by using water and a fertilizer that does not increase the alkalinity (see page 50). You can test the pH of the soil by using a test kit that uses a liquid indicator with a different colour for each step in pH. There are also small electronic devices for the same purpose. If your soil is neutral, you will get a reading of pH = seven, if the soil is acid

The use of ceramic containers greatly improves the presentation of plants like these adromischus.

45

then the reading will be less than seven, and a reading greater than seven indicates that the soil is alkaline, each single number increase representing ten times more acid or alkaline.

Franz Buxbaum first brought the importance of pH to the attention of most cactus growers in his landmark book *Cactus Culture Based on Biology*. Before that time, many species that are easily grown today were grafted because cultivation on their own roots had proved impossible in the alkaline soils growers then used. Buxbaum illustrated the increase in weight in cereus seedlings at various values of pH, proving that the ideal value was about six, that is slightly acid, and that a seedling at neutral hardly grew at all. This result has since been found to be applicable to a wide range of cactus species, particularly those from South America. Some succulents and many cacti from Mexico thrive in soils nearer to neutral but if you aim to maintain your soil at a pH of six, then most species will do perfectly well.

Containers

Only used by a few collectors these days, terracotta pots were once the most popular containers for growing succulents. They are still preferred by some growers for the cultivation of species that are very sensitive to moisture since they dry out quickly. However, they have many disadvantages caused by their porous nature, not least the fact that they are so difficult to clean.

The artistic use of attractive containers with thoughtful planting makes a good show exhibit.

Plastic pots with drainage holes are the popular choice today, being available in a wide range of sizes, shapes and colours. The overall appearance of a collection can be greatly enhanced by using plastic pots of the same colour – some growers choose black or green rather than the usual terracotta. Square pots are available in the smaller sizes and these pack together neatly on the greenhouse benches (see page 41) but no pot less than 6cm (2.5in) in diameter should be used, because anything smaller would dry out too quickly for the plants to thrive.

The main problem for succulent growers is that most pots are only made for short-term use. Disposable pots, made as cheaply as possible, tend to be flimsy with thin walls. Pots are used in a succulent collection for years and so need to be strong and resistant to the degrading effect of sunshine as well having adequate drainage holes.

For larger plants, shallow pots are the best choice since the root systems of succulents tend to be shallow and if there is a lot of unused soil in the bottom of the pot, it will stay wet for too long and lead to problems. For this reason, growers prefer to use half-pots or pans in sizes larger than 10cm (4in) in diameter, but these are getting increasingly difficult to buy.

Attractive glazed pottery containers are very popular in the USA, particularly for showing, and are available in a range of suitable sizes and colours that compliment the plants. For some reason the fashion has not yet spread to Europe, but it is to be hoped that it will come because there is no doubt that a beautiful plant is

A collection of lithops can be housed in a small space using square pots.

enhanced by a stylish pot. Large glazed pots are ideal for succulents like agaves when used as feature plants in the garden. Glazed pans are also good containers for making miniature gardens, which are planted with an artistic mixture of plants and sometimes with ornaments. They may be purchased from garden centres and are often given as presents. Care with watering is needed as they usually have no drainage holes, but at least you don't get water on your window-ledge. Plants can soon outgrow their space in the bowl so individual potting or a bigger bowl will eventually be required.

Labels

Since succulents can often live for a very long time and never get too big, individual plants can remain in a collection for years, even decades. As the collection grows it becomes increasingly important to label the plants, not only to record the name but also to keep track of where the plant came from. With restrictions on plant material collected from the wild becoming ever tighter, what we have in cultivation today becomes even more important.

Serious collectors keep records of all their plants, usually giving them acquisition numbers that are written on the labels. They keep a note of where each plant came from and whether it was grown from seed collected in habitat or if it has any other authentication. This data is invaluable if the plant is ever used for scientific study. However, most people use the standard white plastic labels pushed down the side of the pot. The main difficulty with these is that the marker pens used to write on them are never completely fade-proof and the information slowly disappears under the influence of the sun. To avoid the complete loss of the information, you can write the acquisition number on the end of the label that is pushed under the soil where it will remain readable. A collection with rows of white plastic labels can look rather like a cemetery – so to make the labels less prominent, try using transparent material to write on. Alternatively, you can use a

'T' label where the written panel is horizontal, just resting on the soil, held in place by a vertical point.

Potting

It is often advised that plants should be re-potted every year, but in practice this is too much of a chore for most collectors and not actually necessary so long as the soil structure remains good and the plant is fed regularly. Ideally, a plant should only be re-potted when it has outgrown its container. You will need suitable compost and enough pots in a range of sizes to allow you to move a plant into a larger size as it grows. The increase in pot size should not be too great, since putting a plant into a pot that is too large can lead to problems. Unless the species is a strong grower, it will not fill the new space with roots quickly enough to prevent it remaining wet so risking root rot.

For easy maintenance, it is desirable that all your plants should grow in the same soil mix so that they all behave similarly with respect to such things as the time taken to dry out after watering. So it follows that all new acquisitions should be re-potted prior to being placed in the collection. These new plants could be growing in anything from

Cultivation, Propagation and Display

Bowl gardens are sold in garden centres and supermarkets and are popular with children.

Open beds are useful for tall-growing cacti and have a pleasing appearance.

pure grit to peat, so if you introduced them without re-potting, they would almost certainly lose their roots in a growing regime designed for plants in soil mixes like the ones recommended here (see page 45). Re-potting is also a good idea because it gives you the chance to check for pests and treat any that are found (see page 51).

The recommended method for re-potting is rather different from that used for non-succulent plants and is a major activity for all collectors. The best time to re-pot plants is in warm weather during the growing season but if you have to do it in winter, dry soil should be used and no water should be given until the beginning of the growing season. To handle spiny plants, you may want to wear gloves or you can hold the plant with a strip of folded newspaper wrapped around it.

1. Be sure that the plant you are about to pot is dry then remove the plant from its pot by holding it firmly, turning it upside down, and striking the rim of the pot on the edge of the bench. If it is sticking, try pressing the sides of the pot to loosen it.
2. If the plant's root system is healthy then the root ball will be intact and you can squeeze and shake it to remove the soil. If any of the roots break easily, then they are dead and should be removed. If any major roots are

A raised bed like this takes a lot of maintenance since the plants soon grow into each other.

rotten, cut them off with a clean knife and treat the cut surface with sulphur. Take special care with tuberous-rooted plants not to damage the swollen root because some of these species are very prone to rotting. If you see white masses in the roots and on the inside of the pot then this is root mealy bug and needs to be treated (see page 52).

3. Remove as much soil as you need to in order to ensure that there are no hard lumps of old soil left behind. This is particularly important if you are potting from a peat-based compost. If the roots cannot be extracted from these lumps, it is better to cut them out and treat the cut surfaces with sulphur.

4. Choose the new pot so that there will be a space of about 1–2cm (0.5–1in) around small plants and 3–4cm (1.25–1.5in) around larger ones. Put some compost in the bottom and place the plant in the pot so that the original soil level is about 1cm (0.5in) below the rim of the new pot. The soil will sink slightly after potting anyway, which will leave a space for watering. Spread the roots out and fill in with the new soil, firming lightly with your fingers to hold the plant in place but not enough to fill the air spaces that are so important to the plant's health. Finish off with a thin layer of gravel to fill the pot to near the rim and replace the label.

5. Place the newly potted plant in a warm, shady place and leave it dry for at least a week. When you water for the first time, only water lightly since it will take some time for the roots to penetrate the new soil which should not be allowed to get too wet before the roots grow into it. After a few weeks, the plant can be returned to the collection and treated normally.

When potting strong-growing plants such as the larger cerei, you should give them a much bigger pot than the diameter of the stem base suggests. They will need a full-depth pot to accommodate their extensive root systems.

Raised Planting Beds

A place where plants can be planted out and given a free root run is aesthetically pleasing and can also produce impressive growth. Even in a small glasshouse, a collection of similar plants such as stapeliads or mesembryanthemums can be planted in a large, shallow container on the staging. There is, however, a great deal of expertise involved in making and maintaining these plantings. The most popular types

49

are those created to allow tall-growing species to be planted in a raised bed near to the ground. These must be constructed in the sunniest part of the glasshouse, ideally not shaded by benching. Once the concrete floor is in position, a wall about four bricks high can be built to make a trough. After placing polystyrene insulation in the bottom, the trough should be lined throughout with strong polythene with a few drainage holes. The trough should then be half filled with course grit on to which a layer of sharp sand is placed. It is a good idea to place a thermostatically controlled heating cable in the sand to enable the soil to be kept warm early and late in the season. Finally, the remainder of the trough is filled with the standard mix (see page 45) to which has been added an extra part of grit to give the soil a longer life. The soil in this bed will probably not be replaced for ten years so it needs to keep its structure for that time.

The choice of plants is important: the golden rule is not to mix plants of very different vigour, since they have to compete for water and nutrients and the weaker growers will not thrive. Remember also that large-growing species will soon fill the trough with roots, particularly near the surface, and then they will grow very quickly. Examples of such plants include *Pachycereus pringlei*, *Cleistocactus strausii*, *Echinocactus grusonii*, *Euphorbia ingens*, the larger agaves and aloes, trichocereus, opuntias with large round pads and pereskias. All these can look impressive, but if you want to grow choicer, slower species such as espostoa, haageocereus, ferocactus, tephrocactus or smaller succulents, then leave the fast-growing ones out.

Once the bed has been filled with roots, it will need regular watering and feeding in the growing season (see next paragraph). The soil heating cable can be used in early spring to bring the temperature of the soil up above 20°C (68°F) before the first watering is given, since otherwise, such a large mass of soil would take a long time to heat up enough to stimulate root growth. Some raised beds are constructed with an open bottom so that the plants can root down into the native soil. This suits some species but for others the constant dampness and winter cold can cause problems. On balance, a bed separated and insulated from the ground allows the widest range of species to be grown.

Watering and Feeding

Once you have potted your plants and placed them in the glasshouse, they will need regular watering and feeding. This is a pleasurable activity and gives you the chance to look at your plants and enjoy them. It is often while you are watering that you first notice flower buds appearing or a new offset, but it is also a good opportunity to watch for pests or signs of disease. The earlier you spot a problem and deal with it, the better (see page 51).

The organization of plants in the glasshouse is worth some thought. Some growers put related plants together since this makes the provision of any special treatment they need less time consuming, but others prefer to mix the plants up to create an attractive display. For ease of maintenance, small pots should be kept together where they can be watered more often, probably at least three times more frequently than large pots.

During the growing season, the objective is to provide water soon after the pots have dried out from the previous watering. It is best to thoroughly wet the whole pot of soil each time you water rather than giving them a partial wetting. It takes a lot of practice to perfect this technique since the time taken for a pot to dry out depends on the weather, the vigour of the plant and the size of the pot. If you use the same soil for all plants, experience helps you tell how dry a pot is by picking it up and feeling the weight. It doesn't really matter if you leave plants dry for a while, one of the benefits of growing succulent plants is that they will not die if you leave them dry, they just stop growing and wait. Neither is it a disaster if you water a pot when it is still moist from the last time, but you should avoid making a habit of doing so, and certainly not when the weather is cold in early spring and autumn when particular care is needed.

Once the plant has a good root system spread throughout the pot then regular feeding will be necessary to optimize growth. When plants are growing quickly, they are particularly susceptible to lack of light so be careful not to overfeed late in the year when light levels are falling and the plants need to be hardening off ready for the winter. Generally speaking, most growers don't feed their plants enough – because of the porous nature of the soil used, nutrients are rapidly leached out with watering and the plants will then stop growing. The recommendation is to feed with half-strength liquid fertilizer every time you water established plants from early spring through to late summer. A low-nitrate liquid feed (12.5N-25P-25K) that is acid in solution and contains trace elements is the best one to use. When the plants are growing strongly in spring and early summer then a balanced liquid feed (20N-20P-20K), which has relatively more nitrogen, may be used. This is particularly beneficial to large-growing species, such as cerei and large leafy succulents.

Nitrogen (N) in feeds encourages plants to grow but in excess can lead to weak unnatural growth. Phosphorus (P) encourages flowering and the growth of roots. Potassium (K) strengthens the plant, increasing its resistance to adverse conditions and promotes healthy metabolism. Whichever fertilizer you choose, make sure it has trace elements because these are vital for healthy growth and succulent soils can suffer from deficiencies leading to browning of the growing point and chlorosis.

Because of the great diversity of succulent habitats, there are exceptions to this watering and feeding advice. First, winter-growing succulents need to be watered from late summer through to early spring. This needs to be done carefully in places such as northern Europe where the light levels and temperatures are low. Plants should be put in the brightest place available and allowed to dry out between watering. An even more dilute low-nitrate fertilizer should be used, but only occasionally. The other main exception is for miniature, highly succulent plants such as most of the mesembryanthemums which, as well as having various growing seasons when they need to be watered (see page 167), should only be fed very sparingly, otherwise they tend to grow unnaturally large and bloated.

If your plants stand in watertight trays like those described earlier in this chapter, you have the option of putting the water into the trays and letting the pots take it up. You can only water this way if the soil fills the pot down to the drainage holes, as recommended in this book, and if the trays are reasonably level, since a slope will mean the pots in the lower part of the tray will get most of the water. It takes some practice to gauge the correct amount of water to pour into the tray, but if any remains unused

after half an hour, it should be mopped out as the plants must never be left standing in water for a long time.

Most species can be watered overhead without difficulties, which keeps the plants clean but washes off wool and can leave watermarks on leaves. It is easier to judge the amount of water when applying it individually to each pot, and the excess runs out of the drainage holes. In sealed trays much of this will be sucked back as the soil ingredients absorb it, particularly useful in early spring when first watering dry soil. Some growers spray their plants in the evening to simulate the mist many species benefit from in their natural habitats.

The quality of the water is very important. The best is rainwater, saved from the roof of the glasshouse or your house, so long as there is no possibility of something harmful, such as chemical sprays from nearby farming activities, polluting it. The roof, pipes and storage tank need to be kept clean to avoid the build-up of fungal infections from rotting leaves, dead animals or birds. Rainwater can be stored in a water butt inside the glasshouse and acidified by the addition of a small amount of acidifying agent such as potassium dihydrogen phosphate, which is used in aquaria. The first time you treat the water, you should use a pH indicator or test strip to ascertain the amount to use to adjust the water to pH = 6.

If collecting rainwater is impractical, then tap water can be used, but if you live in a hard water area it will need acidifying to prevent the hardness slowly making the soil in the pots alkaline. This build-up of alkalinity is a major reason for root loss in plants such as gymnocalycium, parodia and rebutia.

Pests and Diseases

Cacti and succulents are not particularly prone to problems but there are a few common pests and diseases that they need to be protected against. Good cultural practices are a great help and top of the list is cleanliness. It is very important to keep your glasshouse clean and tidy. For some reason it is very tempting to put sickly plants under the bench where they will only deteriorate further and probably die. Dead plants are a breeding ground for pests, particularly sciara fly, so you should keep the floor clear of weeds and any other material that will harbour pests. Occasional cleaning of the trays in which the plants stand will also help to reduce problems. The most susceptible to attack by pests and disease are plants that are in a weakened state due to poor culture such as root loss or insufficient light.

Some pests are introduced into the glasshouse from the garden and it is difficult to stop that happening, but one thing you can do is to re-pot and examine all newly acquired plants to make sure there are no unwelcome stowaways in the roots or on the body. Anything that is found should be treated before the plant is put near the rest of your collection. A succulent greenhouse has the sort of climate that allows pests to reproduce at an alarming rate in summer, so you need to be vigilant. If a plant is not growing as it should, knock it out of the pot and see if it has any root disorder such as root mealy bug or root rot. The sooner you find any problem the easier it is to treat and less long-term harm will be caused.

Recent controls on the use of insecticides and fungicides have resulted in fewer chemical controls being approved for amateur use. There is increasing emphasis on more environmentally friendly methods of control such as the use of natural predators for the control of specific pests. The idea is that you build up a balance of predator and pest, where the former has enough food but the latter is reduced in number to such a degree that no serious damage is done. In botanical gardens and large glasshouses, such as those used for commercial production, this approach is achieving good results, but it is more difficult in a small amateur collection. For the average collector, some new, less toxic chemicals are very effective. For those preferring to avoid chemicals altogether, the use of blue or yellow sticky traps (which are really intended to monitor populations) will help to control flying pests.

The following is a list of those pests and diseases most likely to be encountered and the symptoms of their presence. For control agents you are advised to check the current information published by insecticide manufacturers. Always follow the manufacturers' instructions when using chemicals and observe the safety recommendations. Few chemicals are known to have an adverse effect on cacti but some succulents such as crassulaceae may be damaged by organophosphates, so read the label and do a test on a few plants first. It is a common prac-

tice for growers to spray or water with an insecticide a few times in the season as a prophylactic. The only problem with this approach is that the pests can become immune to the insecticide you use, so if you decide to spray regularly, it is a good idea to ring the changes with different categories of insecticide.

Mealy Bug

The commonest insect pest and one that should not be taken lightly since it is capable of rapidly spreading and killing plants. They look like small woodlice, covered in white coating; the most obvious sign of their presence is the mass of white fluffy wax they leave all over the plants. They reproduce quickly and suck the sap of the plants, which are severely damaged and eventually killed. They are particularly difficult to eradicate from between the tightly packed leaves of some succulents. With small infestations, localized application of an insecticide can be sufficient but with a larger outbreak the use of systemic insecticide is more effective. Plants will benefit from a thorough washing afterwards with a jet of water to remove any debris.

Root Mealy Bug

Similar to mealy bugs, these infest the roots and parts of the plant below ground so they are more difficult to detect. The usual indication of their presence is that the plant stops growing and looks pale and sickly. A suspicious plant should be knocked out of its pot and checked. If root mealy bugs are the problem then they will be visible among the roots and on the inside of the pot as bluish-white patches. To treat it, wash as much soil off the roots as possible and stand them in insecticide for an hour or so, then let them dry before potting in new soil. It is a good idea to water nearby plants in the same tray with a systemic insecticide since the root mealy bugs may have spread to these as well.

Spider Mite

Perhaps this is the worst pest because a plant can very quickly be seriously damaged. These tiny red mites can occur in huge numbers and cover a plant with a fine web, particularly when the environment is hot and dry. They damage the epidermis of plants by sucking the sap and the effect is that the tissue turns brown. In the worst cases, the whole plant is covered with this brown scar tissue, which will never recover. Sometimes the plant is killed and in any case it takes a long time to grow out from the damage. Cacti such as rebutia, echinopsis and turbinicarpus are particularly susceptible but all succulents can suffer from this common pest, which can be introduced from plants in your garden.

Western Flower Thrip

This was only introduced to the UK in the late 1980s and many growers are still oblivious to its existence, assuming the damage they see is caused by spider mite. However, it can do extensive damage to the epidermis of plants, particularly soft new tissue and flower parts. The adults are just over 1mm in length, yellow-brown in colour with narrow wings fringed with hairs. The wingless larvae are less than half the adult size, and it is these that feed on the plant epidermis and cause the damage. The life cycle can be as short as twelve days in favourable conditions. The adults are most easily seen by looking in open flowers and they are attracted to blue sticky traps in summer. There is a biological control available and a number of insecticides are effective but at least three repeat treatments are necessary at weekly intervals to achieve good control.

Sciara Fly

Also known as mushroom fly, this is mainly a threat to seedlings. The tiny flies can be seen hovering above the soil, particularly in autumn. They are attracted to rotting plant material and lay their eggs in humus rich-soils where the larvae hatch out and eat plant roots or even whole seedlings from the inside, leaving just a shell. Even older plants can die as a result of rot entering the tissue damaged by the larvae. An appropriate insecticide is the most effective treatment.

White Fly

This is only a problem for some leafy succulents. The tiny white flies attach themselves to the underside of the leaf and take off in a cloud when disturbed. Spraying with a suitable insecticide will control them but they are difficult to eradicate.

Vine Weevil

Now a common problem for gardeners, the larvae of this pest that are mainly found in patio tubs and containers, burrow inside the stems of some succulents such as echeverias and destroy the plant. There are now some specific treatments that are said to very effective against vine weevil and other sap-sucking pests.

Slugs and Snails

Not a problem in a dry glasshouse with a solid floor but given the chance, slugs and snails will eat succulents. If necessary, slug pellets can be used to protect plants, especially seedlings in trays.

Mice

Particularly in the winter, mice will get into the glasshouse and can cause damage to plants. They collect seed pods and will eat plants and even the plastic pots and labels if they are really hungry!

Fungal Infections

Together, these are probably the main cause of the death of succulents in cultivation. The high humidity of the cultural environment leads to a greater prevalence of fungal infections than in the natural habitats, which are much drier. It is not always the degree of cold in the winter that kills plants but the fungi associated with the humidity. After all, many succulents withstand very low temperatures where they grow naturally, but the air is dry.

Various forms of stem rot are a major problem and there is no effective cure. All that can be done is for the damaged tissue to be entirely removed with the blade of a knife, dipped in alcohol after each cut to sterilize it. The vascular ring will often transmit the infection through the plant, so if the ring appears brown this must be cut away in the hope that there will be enough of the plant left to enable it to be rooted as a cutting. Cut surfaces should be treated with sulphur powder, left to dry for a few days in a warm, shady place then rooted like a cutting. Fruits or flower remains can sometimes become infected and rot back into the plant, particularly late in the season, so all fruits and dead flowers should be removed as soon as they can easily be detached.

Rotting of the roots will stop a plant growing and may even spread into the body and cause death. Alkalinity, overdue potting, insect infestation or over-watering usually causes this. The plant should be removed from the pot, all rotting roots cut back to healthy tissue and

This ripe gymnocalycium fruit has split to reveal the seeds that are ready to harvest.

treated with sulphur. After a few days of drying in a warm, shady place, it can be rooted like a cutting.

Damping off is probably the greatest threat faced by seedlings. It is recommended that the soil be soaked in a suitable fungicide before sowing since the seeds themselves can carry fungus spores if they have not been properly washed. However, some fungicides are based on copper and should not be used because they are highly alkaline in solution and may inhibit germination.

Viruses

Most collectors give little or no thought to viruses but they can cause problems in a succulent collection. The symptoms of a plant with a harmful virus are usually poor and distorted growth, a blotchy epidermis or distorted flowers. There is no cure, so if a plant exhibits any of these symptoms for a long time, it should be destroyed and replaced since it risks infecting others. Viruses are spread by the activities of biting insects that pass them from plant to plant. Grafting on to infected stocks can also spread them. You should never graft on to stocks that have formed as offsets under other grafts since these may be infected. Always use seedlings or the tops off these after using them for grafting since these will not have come into contact with another plant.

Propagation

One of the most rewarding things about collecting and growing plants is that you can always make more individuals by propagation. You will also be making an important practical contribution to conservation, and selling spare plants not only helps other collectors but the money can go towards your expenses such as heating, pots, soil and so on. For growers of fuchsias, dahlias, roses and many other garden plants, there are always new hybrids coming on to the market or you can make your own, but with succulents it is the true species that are most in demand, particularly if they have some provenance – pedigree if you like.

Succulent enthusiasts are always looking for plants belonging to newly discovered species, so to reduce the temptation to steal plants illegally from the wild, skilled propagators endeavour to satisfy the demand by using a number of techniques. Increasingly popular for those species that are difficult to propagate by traditional methods is tissue culture, where a small piece of one individual can be artificially grown under laboratory conditions on a suitable medium in a flask. This formless mass of cells can eventually be stimulated to produce normal growth that can be transferred into the usual cultural conditions. This is not a technique that the average hobbyist can easily use, but it is proving useful for multiplying the numbers of a species that cannot be readily propagated by seed or cuttings. Plants produced by tissue culture are genetically identical so it results in many plants in cultivation being of the same clone.

Seed Raising

Probably the most satisfying aspect of the hobby is seed raising. If the seed is from the wild or a number of cultivated plants, then the seedlings may be remarkably diverse, and it is only through raising seeds that you can appreciate the variation in a species. For instance, as a batch of lithops seedlings develop their patterns there will probably be no two that are identical.

Seed raising has a reputation for being difficult, but so long as a few simple principals are followed, results can be very satisfactory. The first thing is to start with good seed, which you can either collect from your plants or buy from a dealer (see page Appendix I). Your own seed will often germinate best because you can sow it fresh, but of course you only get more of the plants you already have. In most cases you will also need two plants of the same species to set seed, but they do not necessarily need to flower at the same time. You can collect the pollen, seal it in foil to keep it dry, and store it in a refrigerator until a flower on another plant opens.

Pollination of cactus flowers is usually easy to do by transferring the pollen from the stamens of one flower to the stigma of one on another plant. It is worth repeating the exercise at different times of the day since flowers are not always receptive, even when they are open. Some succulents, such as haworthia, produce a flower spike where the flowers open progressively up the stalk. To pollinate these

you should cross older flowers with ones that have just opened, since ripe pollen and a receptive stigma occur at different times of a flower's life. Pollination can also be affected by temperature or humidity so that pollination in cultivation can sometimes be difficult to achieve. The most difficult succulents to set fruit on are stapeliads and some other *Ascepiadaceae* where the flowers have a complex mechanism evolved for pollination by specific insects. They can sometimes produce their seed horns spontaneously and it has been said that this can be encouraged by putting the flowering plants outside in the garden where presumably some insect can do the job.

Cactus seedlings at a few weeks old are already growing spines.

After a few months, cactus seedlings start to look like tiny adult plants.

At about one year old, the seedlings are ready to prick out into trays.

Seeds can be stored in cool, dry conditions for some time, even many years in some cases. Little scientific research has been done on the time seeds remain viable but as a general rule they are best sown within two years. Some large seeds such as astrophytum, frailea, and opuntias appear to lose their viability quickly whilst very small seeds like lithops still germinate well after ten years or more. The seeds of some genera, for example lobivia, germinate better after they have been stored for over a year than they do if sown in the year after harvest. This variation probably accounts for the inconsistent results obtained from seeds bought from dealers, who usually supply seeds from several years' harvests.

Once the pods are ripe the seed should be harvested, washed and dried. With some genera it can take a long time for seed pods to appear. In mammillaria, for example, the pods of most species may be pushed out of the plant body up to a year after flowering, whilst in others such as *M. theresae* and *M. perezdelarosae*, they are never clearly visible and have to be practically dug out of the plant. Some fruits are dry and the seeds can literally be poured out, whilst others are full of sticky pulp that needs to be softened in water then sieved and dried to release the seeds.

The best time to sow most seeds is in spring when a daytime temperature of 20–25°C (68–77°F) should lead to good germination. This temperature can be provided by artificial heating such as soil cables in sand under the trays or simply by waiting until early May when the sun will do the job for you. If you want to sow seed very early in the year, then as well as artificial heating, you may need to provide artificial light by positioning a bank of fluorescent tubes a few inches above the soil. This is a lot of trouble and expense if you just want to raise a few seeds, so such an approach is probably best left until you become an avid seed raiser.

Cactus seedlings pricked out and in their third growing season, some are already flowering.

Seedling production by the million under polythene in southern California.

Some growers like to sow mesembryanthemum seed in the autumn, which is probably the best time to sow winter-growing succulents as well.

The containers can either be small pots or seed trays divided up into segments for each seed batch. The latter are easier to keep evenly moist since the larger volume of soil dries out more slowly. The most suitable commercial seed composts are those made from fine peat or peat substitute to which can be added some fine vermiculite or perlite. Having filled the container, a thin layer of grit should be placed over the top. The best type to use are lime-free round pebbles of about 2–3mm in diameter and the layer should be about one pebble deep. This gives the seeds a place to settle where they still receive light, which is necessary for germination, and some protection from drying of the compost surface. As the seeds grow, the gravel will also reduce the tendency for moss to develop. The tray should be soaked in tap water and drained, then the seeds sown thinly so that the resulting seedlings can be left undisturbed for up to a year without overcrowding. If they become packed together there is a greater chance of fungal infections and moving them too young may lead to losses. If sowing in trays, it is best to segregate the fast-growing species from slower ones.

Once sown, the seeds need to be lightly sprayed with a fungicide such as chinosol to wash them into the gravel where they can germinate. To maximize germination, the seeds need to be kept in a humid atmosphere, so the tray should be placed under a tight-fitting sheet of white (not clear) polythene that needs to be only a few centimetres above the soil. Although the tray should be put in a bright place in the greenhouse, it must be protected from direct

Seedlings of Discocactus zehntneri in California – practical conservation in action.

sun. Daytime temperatures above 20°C (68°F) are necessary for success but night temperatures should be lower. This variation encourages germination, which will occur at any time from a few days through to a few weeks depending on the species and the freshness of the seed. During this time no action is necessary other than an occasional check to see that there is no fungal rot in the seedlings. The white polythene can be left in place until all the seeds that are likely to germinate have done so, and then it can be raised like a tent to give more air. In summer this should be replaced by fleece to allow more air movement while still maintaining some higher humidity. Once this stage is reached, the seedlings should look like miniature versions of what they will eventually grow into and they will need watering to keep the compost just moist.

During the first winter the seedlings should be lightly watered in fine weather to stop them drying out. When the new growing season starts around April, the young plants will start to grow rapidly, at which time they can be pricked out into another tray of normal cactus compost for growing on. Light shade is still desirable until their third year when they can be treated as adult plants.

There is a wide variety in the growth rate of different seedlings and some of the quicker ones, like many succulents, will need to be removed from the polythene cover and pricked out much sooner than described above. The first individual pots should be no smaller than 6cm (2.5in) in diameter since smaller pots dry out too quickly for good growth to be achieved. If you continue to keep these pots segregated in a seedling area of the greenhouse, then placing them on capillary matting increases the time between waterings and produces better results with all but those plants that are very sensitive to moisture.

Cuttings

For many plants, propagation by cuttings is a good way of increasing your stock and the only way to guarantee that the characteristics of a hybrid will be perpetuated, since cuttings are genetically identical to the plant they were removed from. If a plant produces offsets or side-shoots naturally, then these can be cut off and rooted as cuttings. Some species naturally form clumps where the new plants around the edge already have their own root systems. These can be removed, potted up straight away and treated as normal plants. This is the best way to propagate many haworthias, gasterias, some aloes and a number of cacti. If, for instance, a cactus is naturally solitary then the growing point can be cut out, which will result in the production of offsets that will make cuttings. It can then become a stock plant that will continue to produce cuttings for years. Rooting leaves that will then produce small plants from their bases, which can be removed and grown on, are a convenient way to propagate leaf succulents such as haworthia, gasteria, adromischus and echeveria.

When taking a cutting, always cut in the place that leaves the smallest cut surface possible, such as the junction of an offset with the main stem. Unlike ordinary plants, cuttings of succu-

Use a sharp knife to take a cutting at the narrowest part of the stem.

Offsets can be removed using a sharp knife and make excellent cuttings.

lents will not wilt and die if kept dry but if watered immediately may well rot. Cut surfaces should therefore be dusted with sulphur and left to dry for a few days in a warm, shady place to form a callous before being placed on a rooting medium such a mixture of grit and perlite that should be kept moist and warm. Large cut surfaces, however, may require weeks before they are healed enough to prevent rotting. In a few weeks, roots will be formed from the vascular bundles or, in the case of some cacti, from areoles near the cut, then the plant can be potted in the usual way. When taking cuttings of euphorbias, care must be taken to avoid contact with the milky sap, which can be very unpleasant if brought into contact with sensitive parts of the body such as the eyes. Cuttings can be stood in water for a few moments to stop the sap bleeding from the cut surface. Some succulents, such as *Pachypodium succulentum*, can be grown from pieces of their fattened roots, but this is the least common type of cutting.

Grafting

This technique can be used not only to increase clones of slow-growing or rare plants, but also as a permanent cultural method for cacti and some other succulents that are difficult or impossible to grow on their own roots in the environment available. For permanent grafts you want to make the plant look as natural as possible, as if it was on its own roots. It is a good idea to use a short stock since this will change the natural appearance of the scion less than a larger one, which will tend to make it look bloated or just too big to be natural. Fundamentally, the more green tissue of the stock there is above ground, the more the scion will be pumped up, which is fine for rapid propagation but not desirable for long-term culture. Short stocks can eventually be buried so improving the appearance of the plant, whilst retaining the benefit of the strong and reliable roots of the stock. This cultural method can be used for any plant and was once used for whole collections of cacti, particularly in mainland Europe, but now it tends to be restricted to a few difficult genera such as sclerocactus, pediocactus, discocactus and some euphorbias.

Recommended stocks for particular purposes:

Dust the cut surfaces with sulphur and leave to dry for a few days before rooting.

- Seedlings for later re-grafting on a permanent stock: hylocereus* pereskiopsis or echinopsis;
- Permanent grafting of a wide range of species: trichocereus or echinopsis;
- Permanent grafting where strong spination is desired: *Harrisia jusbertii*;
- Permanent grafting of hardy species where the winter temperature will be below freezing: hardy echinocereus such as *E. chloranthus*;
- Choice opuntias: *O. cylindrica* or another opuntia;
- Euphorbias: *E. canariensis*.

*Hylocereus needs to be kept warm throughout the year so is best restricted to heated propagation facilities. If you buy a plant grafted on hylocereus (recognizable by its three-ribbed stems) you will have to keep it warm or re-graft the plant on something hardier.

Suitable plants for grafting are small, usually offsets or young plants. A very useful but trickier type of grafting utilizes seedlings that are only a few days old. These are grafted on to small pieces of pereskiopsis or hylocereus and, if a bit older, on to echinopsis (see diagram 3). This specialist technique is not described in detail here, but once grafting of larger plants is mastered, it is fun to try. The grafted seedlings will grow very quickly and the top half of them can soon be permanently grafted leaving the base to produce offsets for further propagation. In this way a single seed can result in dozens of plants within a year

A grafted cactus. The top is the scion; the bottom plant is the stock.

1. Vascular bundles of stock and scion match perfectly.

2. A smaller scion offset on a larger stock to ensure union.

3. A young plant or small cutting placed on the vascular ring of the stock.

or so, an excellent way to make new discoveries available and reduce the desire to collect plants from the wild.

Grafted plants need to be treated in a way that suits the stock; so a little water in winter will help to stop excessive dehydration, which can cause the stock to die – this is a particular problem with echinopsis. A problem with grafted plants is that the stock will often grow shoots (known as suckers) that must be removed to stop them taking over from the graft. One way to stop this happening is to rub off all the areoles from the stock, but care must be taken to ensure that the wounds heal very thoroughly before the stock is buried.

Never be tempted to use removed suckers as stocks for other grafts because they may contain a virus that would spread to a new graft. The best way is to grow stocks from seed and then, so long as you keep your knife sterilized in spirit, you can re-root the top part removed during grafting and use it again.

The best time to do grafting is in warm weather when the plants are in active growth. The best results will be obtained when stock and scion are turgid, that is full of sap and not soft. You will need a sharp thin-bladed knife like a scalpel, some spirit to sterilize it, potted stocks and some rubber bands. Inside the stems of most cacti there is a ring of vascular bundles and it is these that need to unite between stock and scion for a graft to take. It follows therefore that the best grafts are produced when the diameter of the vascular ring of the two plants is the same (see diagram 1). If they are different, then you must offset the scion on the stock to ensure that the rings cross (see diagram 2). Cristates have their bundles in a parallel pair of lines, so the stock needs to be large enough for these lines to cross the stock's vascular ring in four places.

The procedure is as follows:

1. Make a straight cut across the stock and remove the top part.
2. Bevel the edges so that when the cut surface dries and the centre sinks, the scion is not pushed off by the epidermis, which does not shrink.
3. Make a further cut across the vascular ring with a single action so that the surface will be flat and leave the slice in place to keep the cut moist.

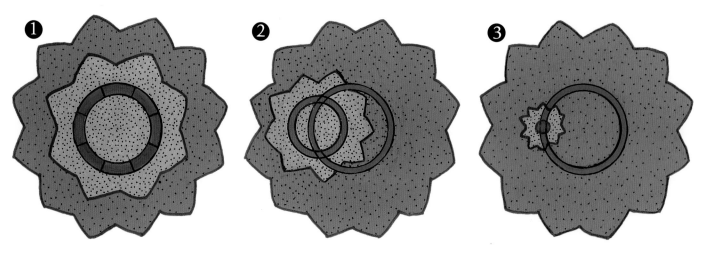

❶   ❷   ❸

4. Prepare the scion by making a clean cut across it. The edges need only be bevelled if the cut surface is large or the epidermis is particularly tough.

5. Remove the protective slice off the stock and place the scion on to the cut surface. With light pressure, rub the scion over the surface to exclude any air bubbles, remove excess sap and ensure intimate contact between the surfaces.

6. Stretch a suitably sized elastic band under the pot and over the top of the scion so that it applies firm pressure to hold it in place. With soft scions it may be necessary to place some padding under the band to stop it causing damage. A second band should then be placed at right angles to the first. If you do a lot of grafting you can make a frame with sprung steel clips that can be used to apply the pressure in place of bands.

7. Place the grafted plant in a warm place out of direct sunlight but with free air movement so that the cut surfaces can dry and heal. The stock should be watered and the bands left on for about three days after which the graft should have taken.

Cut the stock with a sharp knife or razor blade.

Bevel the edges of the stock.

Cut the scion off the parent plant.

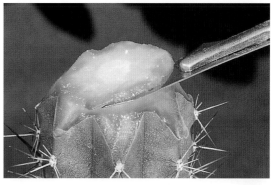

Take a thin slice off the stock and leave it in place.

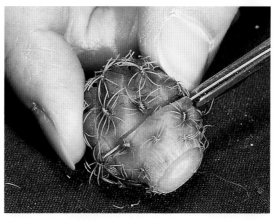

Prepare the scion by making a single, clean cut.

Remove the loose slice from the stock and place the scion on top.

Press gently and rub the scion over the stock to remove air.

Place a rubber band over the top.

Place a second rubber band over the scion.

A 'grafting machine', comprising sprung steel arms can be used instead of rubber bands.

If the scion subsequently falls off or fails to grow, you can re-do the graft with new cuts. With practice, a high proportion of success will be achieved, particularly as you get quicker and reduce the opportunity for the surfaces to partly dry before being placed together. If the cutting of the scion leaves a reasonable sized piece below the cut then that piece can be grafted in the same way but upside-down. Since this piece will have no growing point, it will produce shoots from the areoles that are perfect for further grafting or rooting as cuttings.

Variations of the above technique can be used for scions of different shapes. For instance, the flat stems of some epiphytic cacti can be grafted by cutting them into a wedge-shape and inserting them into a slot cut in the stock. A slanting cut can be made across thin-stemmed scions so that the vascular bundle is oval-shaped and so large enough to be easily grafted on standard stocks. When grafting euphorbias, you must wait for the cuts to stop bleeding before introducing the surfaces together. Be very careful to avoid getting the milky sap on your skin and particularly on sensitive parts of the body such as the eyes.

4 Which Species to Choose - Cacti

Astrophytum

This is a very popular genus with just four species, all from Mexico and the far south of the USA. There are few collections without at least one example of these beautiful plants. As well as the species, there are many cultivated hybrids that have been selected for specific characteristics, particularly the patterns of white flecks that decorate the green bodies.

All astrophytums enjoy hot, sunny conditions with less than average water in the summer and cool, dry winters. Although they grow well in the normal Mexican mix (see page 45) it takes many years to produce the large specimens so popular on the show bench. The seeds are large and fragile, so need to be protected to avoid damage. They keep less well than most cactus seed and need to be sown within a year or so of harvesting for a reasonable percentage to germinate.

Astrophytum capricorne, *a popular species with beautiful flowers.*

Astrophytum asterias, *the smallest and choicest species.*

BELOW: An outdoor plant sale in California, USA.

ASTROPHYTUM ASTERIAS

A. asterias is the smallest species of the genus. The solitary body has about eight broad flat ribs with white flecks and woolly areoles down the middle but no visible spines, and the yellow flowers are freely produced from the young areoles near the centre. It is the most difficult species to cultivate and must be treated with care. It is often grafted on a small piece of echinopsis when young, which can produce excellent specimens, but grafted plants have a tendency to grow tall if they are grown too quickly. *A. asterias* is slow growing and should be given less water than average. Flowers can be expected when the plant is about 3cm (1in) in diameter and it will eventually grow to 10cm (4in) in diameter.

Beautifully marked specimens of this species are avidly collected by the Japanese and epitomized by the remarkable strain known as 'Super Kabuto'. Originally occurring among normal plants, this exceptional form produces a proportion of similar seedlings in its offspring so is now quite widely available. Outstanding individuals can be sold for huge sums of money in Japan where the hobby has an enthusiastic following.

ASTROPHYTUM CAPRICORNE

A group of astrophytums in pots up to 7cm (2.75in) in diameter showing their free-flowering nature.

A variable species from the point of view of the spines, which can be thin and flexible or stout and rigid, black or straw coloured. The solitary body is usually covered in white flecks but can be naked, has about eight ribs and is initially

Astrophytum myriostigma cv. *'Green Square', a four-ribbed selection from the variety nudum.*

globular but becomes short columnar in later life. The spectacular and large yellow flowers have a striking red throat in some forms, and are freely produced from the crown of the plant when it reaches about 5cm (2in) in diameter.

ASTROPHYTUM MYRIOSTIGMA

A very popular plant because of its remarkable appearance. The spineless solitary bodies usually have five ribs but a form with four ribs known as forma quadricostata is highly prized by collectors. Unfortunately, it has a tendency to grow a fifth rib when it gets older. Most plants have a covering of white flecks on the body but the forma nuda is naked and usually has smaller flowers. It is a slow-growing plant and perfect mature specimens are highly rated at shows. It will first flower when about 6cm (2.5in) in diameter and as it gets older it may become columnar, eventually reaching 20cm (8in) in height. *A. myriostigma* requires careful watering at all times and the sunniest position available.

Similar species: *A. coahuilense*

ASTROPHYTUM ORNATUM

The largest and fastest-growing species, *A. ornatum*, when fully mature, can reach a height of over 1m (3ft) in some of its habitats. It has even been suggested that it evolved from hybridization with a ferocactus. Easy to grow, the plant body remains solitary but soon

Astrophytum ornatum, *the biggest species of the genus.*

becomes columnar. It has around eight sharp ribs, the areoles armed with strong golden spines and the large yellow flowers appear at the crown of the plant. Given regular re-potting and usual watering it soon grows into an impressive specimen and will first flower when about 10cm (4in) in diameter.

Columnar Cacti

Hundreds of cactus species are columnar (cereoid) rather than globular, ranging from huge trees weighing tons to miniatures, upright growing to sprawling. They add another dimension to a collection in much the same way as trees do in a garden. Rows of globular cacti on the greenhouse bench can look rather repetitive, so breaking them up with taller plants, perhaps as a backdrop, can look really good. Many columnar cacti are grown for their attractive spination or shape rather than flowers, which may only be produced on specimens so large that they probably would not fit in the greenhouse. The

familiar cactus of the 'Wild West', the saguaro or *Carnegiea gigantea* (see page 17), is a good example of a species unsuitable for glasshouse culture. It is unimpressive as a small plant, slow growing, and cannot be expected to flower. However, there are a number of small-growing species that will easily flower in small pots and give you the best of both worlds. White-spined cacti are always popular and the mainly columnar espostoa and oreocereus are favourite genera for often having copious white hair. In their natural habitats this is protection against the intense sunshine but is still produced easily in cultivation.

A common fault when cultivating cereoid species is the use of pots which are too small although the diameter of the neck of the plant at soil level appears to fit them comfortably. The root system of these plants is extensive and to grow properly it needs space to expand. Planting robust species in a free root run bed in the greenhouse can result in dramatically increased growth rates and success with flowering the larger species.

From the large choice available, the following is a selection for the hobbyist based on various desirable characteristics:

Astrophytum myriostigma, *the classic spineless 'Star Cactus'.*

- Espostoa, oreocereus and cephalocereus for white hair
- Cleistocactus for easy culture and flowers
- Haageocereus for their colourful spination
- Micranthocereus and arrojadoa for their interesting mode of growth and flowers
- Pilosocereus for the remarkable blue epidermis of many species
- Pygmaeocereus for sweet-smelling nocturnal flowers on small plants

ESPOSTOA MELANOSTELE

One of the smallest of the genus that is popular because of the dense white hairs that cover the stems of most species. When young, it looks just like a shaving brush, and it takes many years to reach a maximum height of 1.5m (5ft) by which time it will have branched from the base. In practice, glasshouse grown subjects never get this large, this can only be achieved in outdoor plantings in suitable climates. The white, nocturnal flowers, rarely seen in cultivation, are produced from a cephalium; a special area of the plant modified specifically for the production of flowers, and consisting of a vertical groove filled with long orange wool. A warm, sunny location and average watering suits this plant, which gives no problem in cultivation, it is just slow growing. Its natural habitat in the valleys of western Peru is very dry.

Similar species: *E. lanata, E. nana, E. frutescens*

Espostoa melanostele, *covered in thick wool to protect it from the sun.*

ESPOSTOA SENILIS

Also covered with dense white hairs, this beautiful species is faster growing than *E. melanostele* but requires more water and warmth in cultivation, a minimum temperature of 10°C (50°F) in winter being adequate. The stems are more slender and the branches are formed further up the stem. It has nocturnal pink flowers that are produced from a cephalium rather different from that of *E. melanostele*, being superficial and comprising long bristles that develop near the top of the stem and eventually envelop the crown. When young, the base of the stem develops longer hair-like spines, presumably for protection. It grows to 2m (6.5ft) in height and will begin

Espostoa senilis, *a night-flowering species with unusual pink flowers.*

to flower in a greenhouse at about 1.5m (5ft) so long as the light is good. It comes from the warm, moist valleys to the east of the main Andes mountain range in northern Peru.

Similar species: *E. blossfeldiorum*

OREOCEREUS TROLLII

In contrast to the above, this is an alpine plant, thriving in the high altiplano of northern Argentina and Bolivia. This species grows slowly, eventually making a clump of low stems, each with a dense covering of white hairs penetrated by yellow or red spines. The tubular red flowers are produced from the side of the stem near the top and are evolved for pollination by humming-birds. The flowers appear when the plant is about 60cm (24in) in height, but are only occasionally seen in cultivation because it takes many years to grow to this size. In a sunny location it is easy to cultivate from seeds and can stand freezing conditions in winter so long as it is dry. All other species of oreocereus look similar to this one except for *O. hempelianus*, which looks more like a matucana due to its lack of hair.

Similar species: *O. celsianus, O. leucotrichus*

Oreocereus doelzianus *ssp.* sericatus *with its humming-bird pollinated flowers.*

Oreocereus trollii *from the high mountains of the Andes.*

OREOCEREUS DOELZIANUS SSP. SERICATUS

Another hairy cereoid, this soon forms clusters of slim stems that grow to only 40cm (16in) in height, at which point it grows a bristly terminal cephalium from which the red flowers emerge. The growth of a cephalium differentiates this species from other oreocerei and as a result, it was placed in its own genus, morawetzia, a name often still used today. Easily raised from seed or cuttings, flowering is relatively straightforward to achieve in cultivation and the contrast of the bright red flowers against the white stem makes this subspecies a worthy addition to a collection. The species itself is similar to this sub-species but larger in all respects and with less hair on the stems. They come from the Rio Montaro valley of central Peru.

Cephalocereus
senilis, *the 'Old man
Cactus' from Mexico.*

CEPHALOCEREUS SENILIS

One species of a genus that comes from Mexico, all of which are very large and are grown for their statuesque appearance, since flowering can only be achieved in outdoor plantings in suitable climates. The outstanding feature of *C. senilis* is the long hair on the stem. Although it is very slow growing in cultivation, it can grow to 15m (49ft) tall and 40cm (16in) thick in habitat. When mature it will grow a cephalium from which the whitish nocturnal flowers are produced. It makes spectacular forests on hillsides in Hidalgo, Mexico and has always been very popular with collectors. It can only be grown from seed which, until recently, was always collected in habitat, a process that resulted in extensive damage being done to the plants whilst harvesting the fruits from high up on the stems. Easy to grow in a sunny place with less than average water but much patience is required to grow a specimen taller than 30cm (12in).

Cleistocactus

OPPOSITE:
Cleistocactus
candelilla *produces
hundreds of flowers in
a season.*

This genus includes many species, all of which make good glasshouse plants because of their easy culture and free flowering. The flowers are usually tubular and are pollinated by hummingbirds that are attracted by the copious nectar at the bottom of the flower. They come from the Andes and thrive in the inland valleys that receive regular summer rainfall. Among the easiest of cacti to grow, they need to have a constant supply of moisture in the summer to keep them growing and flowering. Many are capable of flowering several times during the growing season when they can be quite spectacular, particularly if given adequate root room. Some growers experience problems with the growing tips dying, even when young. This is usually due to the plant having too small a pot or being inadequately watered. However, there are some clones that are prone to this and it is best to replace these.

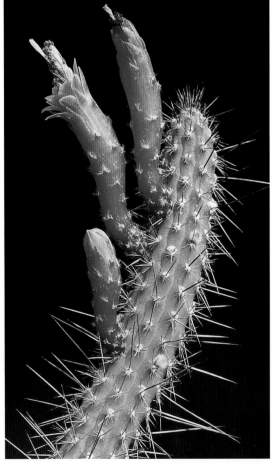

Cleistocactus
baumannii *ssp.*
chacoanus *is very easy
to flower.*

CLEISTOCACTUS STRAUSII

One of the larger species, growing to over 1m (3ft) in height with thick stems that eventually form a clump, branching from the base and covered with white spines. Although it needs to be larger than most before it produces its

maroon flowers, it is one of the most popular of all columnar cacti and is easily raised from seed. It comes from Bolivia.

Similar species: *C. hyalacanthus*

CLEISTOCACTUS BAUMANNII SSP. CHACOANUS

One of the sprawling species with thin stems, this subspecies of the widespread *C. baumannii* has the S-shaped flowers characteristic of the species. It is very easy to grow but tends to look

Cleistocactus strausii, a white-spined species from Bolivia.

Cleistocactus brookeae *is an uncommon plant with unusual flowers.*

untidy in the collection if not staked. As with many cleistocacti, the flowers are produced in profusion: the dead ones just fall off so need to be regularly tidied up. It needs plenty of water in the summer when it will flower for months, and will probably benefit from the occasional pruning to keep it in check and provide cuttings for propagation.

CLEISTOCACTUS CANDELILLA

A very floriferous plant from Bolivia with thin stems that remain upright and branch freely from the base. Easy to raise from seed or cuttings, the same cultural treatment as described above will suit this undemanding plant, which is particularly suited to growing in an open bed in the glasshouse where the free root run will encourage rapid growth and spectacular flower displays.

Similar species: *C. dependens, C. smaragdiflorus*

CLEISTOCACTUS BROOKEAE

One of the best of all cleistocactus species to grow, this outstanding plant combines an attractive spination with curiously shaped flowers of a contrasting red-orange colour. The flowers are produced all through the summer as long as there is moisture at the root; a well-grown plant of 25cm (10in) in height can have over 200 flowers in a season. It is sometimes available as rooted cuttings but can be difficult to find in nursery catalogues since there are only a few clones in cultivation. It branches from the base but its habit is rather lax so may need staking for the best effect. Its close relative, *C. brookeae* ssp. *vulpis-cauda* has similar but darker flowers and its trailing stems make it a perfect subject for a hanging basket.

CLEISTOCACTUS SAMAIPATANUS

This free-flowering species comes from eastern Bolivia and is probably better known as *Bolivicereus samaipatanus*. It is easy to cultivate and with regular watering during the summer it will grow rapidly and regularly produce its dramatic flowers. It is usually offered as cuttings and there is some variation in the clones available in the trade, most being rather lax in habit, but if you can find a strong, upright one you will have an easier plant to manage. Spination is variable, as are the flowers that in some clones have a pale edge to the petals. The stems branch and can be more than 1m (3ft) long, forming thickets if given space to grow.

CLEISTOCACTUS NEOROEZLII

This species from northern Peru forms clumps of stems up to 1m (3ft) in height, branching from the base. The red tubular flowers are produced in flushes from the newer areoles near the crown. Not very often seen for sale, you may find it under the name *Seticereus roezlii* in some lists. Since it comes from the warm inland valleys of northern Peru, it needs to be kept at 10°C (50°F) or more in the winter but otherwise is as easy to grow as any other cleistocactus, being easily raised from seed and enjoying a good-sized pot with adequate water in summer.

Cleistocactus samaipatanus *flowers all through the summer.*

Cleistocactus neoroezlii *relies on humming-birds to pollinate its tubular flowers.*

BELOW: Cleistocactus winteri *is a good choice for a hanging basket.*

CLEISTOCACTUS WINTERI

One of the best plants for a hanging basket in the greenhouse, this very individual plant can be relied upon to flower regularly all through the summer if watered frequently. Better known as *Hildewintera aureispina*, it has curiously shaped flowers with an inner structure unique in the family *Cactaceae*. The slim pendant stems are covered in golden-yellow spines and the pink or orange flowers are borne on the upper sides. Usually grown from cuttings, which root easily and rapidly grow into a well-branched group of stems. It comes from Bolivia where it hangs down cliffs.

HAAGEOCEREUS PSEUDOMELANOSTELE

This species is typical of many haageocerei in cultivation with thick stems branching from the base and a covering of dense golden spines that are particularly pleasing in a mixed collection. The nocturnal flowers can be white or red but are only occasionally seen on cultivated plants, which usually need to be over 25cm (10in) in height before they bloom and then only if given

Haageocereus pacalaensis *from Peru has white, nocturnal flowers.*

a sunny location. All haageocerei are easy to grow in a sunny position with less than average water. Seed is readily available and is the usual method of propagation. Their natural habitat is the dry coastal valleys of central Peru where the spination is much more dense than found in cultivation.

Similar species: *H. acranthus*

HAAGEOCEREUS PACALAENSIS

Similar to the above but with less dense spination, this species comes from valleys further north in Peru. It is smaller growing and only has a white flower, which although nocturnal, remains open in the early morning like many other night-blooming cacti. Treated in the way described for *H. pseudomelanostele*, you may be lucky and see a flower but they are never abundantly produced.

Similar species: *H. repens*

Haageocereus pseudomelanostele *is covered in golden spines like many haageocerei.*

ARROJADOA RHODANTHA

There are many unusual cerei from Brazil and this is an outstanding example. The stems are about 3cm (1in) thick and form a cephalium of long bristles when they have reached around 20cm (8in) in height. The pink, thick-walled, tubular flowers are produced from this cephalium and open in the afternoon and early evening for humming-birds to pollinate them in their natural home. In subsequent growth periods, the stem can continue to grow through the cephalium leaving it behind like a collar and making a new one at the stem apex, a process that can be repeated several times and the stem may grow to 1m (3ft) in length. The old cephalia will continue to flower even after new ones are formed. Stephanocereus is the only other genus that behaves in this way. In cultivation, it is usually grown from seed, requiring a minimum temperature of 10°C (50°F) in winter and normal watering in summer when it enjoys high temperatures. Growing and flowering tends to happen most in late summer and autumn. In its Brazilian homeland it usually grows on flat ground under trees or in rocky places in the caatinga forest.

ARROJADOA PENICILLATA

Although similar to *A. rhodantha*, this species has much more slender stems and tends to clamber through bushes rather than being self-supporting. The stems can grow to 2m (6.5ft) in length but are only 1.5cm (0.5in) thick until they are about to make a cephalium when the stem apex thickens into a club-shape. Easy to grow, this species will flower when only three years old and about 25cm (10in) in height. Stems will continue to flower from the same cephalium for a number of years and only sometimes will they grow through it, often preferring to grow a branch somewhere along the old stem which will go on to flower. Raising seed presents no difficulty and cuttings can be taken, but these can dry up before rooting because they are so thin. Its natural habitat is south-east Brazil in the caatinga forest, where it can be difficult to spot clambering through bushes.

MICRANTHOCEREUS POLYANTHUS

Another interesting plant from Brazil and one where flowers can begin to appear on a single stem just 15cm (6in) in length. The flowers are usually produced in September from a modified zone on one side of the stem where the areoles develop extra bristles. These small, tubular flowers are produced in large numbers, probably for pollination by humming-birds. They are bi-coloured with pink on the outer petals and white inside. The resulting fruits are small, red when ripe, and contain black seeds in a pulp. The seeds are easy to raise, so long as they are kept warm, and the young seedlings quickly grow into attractive plants, the soft yellowish spines and hair almost obscuring the pale blue body of the plant. The stems cluster at the base and grow ultimately to about 70cm (27.5in) in height. Grafting is commonly used to accelerate the development of seedlings, particularly in continental Europe, and the resulting plants are indistinguishable from those on their own roots. A minimum temperature of 10°C (50°F) in winter and a bright situation suits all micran-thocerei.

Similar species: *M. flaviflorus*

Arrojadoa rhodantha *has special flowering zones called cephalia.*

73

Arrojadoa penicillata *from Brazil grows long thin stems that clamber through bushes.*

Pilosocereus

Pilosocereus has many species in Brazil, Mexico and the Caribbean region. They all need some warmth in winter and nearly all grow into trees, so they are only suitable for larger glasshouses where a temperature of at least 10°C (50°F) is maintained. The most attractive are those with a blue epidermis like the species illustrated, which can flower when just 1.5m (5ft) in height although some clones take longer. They will grow quickly providing they are given plenty of root space and a good supply of water in summer.

PILOSOCEREUS PACHYCLADUS

P. pachycladus is widespread in Brazil where it can dominate hillsides with its much branched tree-like form, so seed is widely available and the seedlings soon become a beautiful blue colour that contrasts with the yellow spines. If the plant gets too tall it is possible to cut off the top 30cm (12in) or so and treat it as a

Micranthocereus polyanthus *has many small flowers crowded down one side of the stem.*

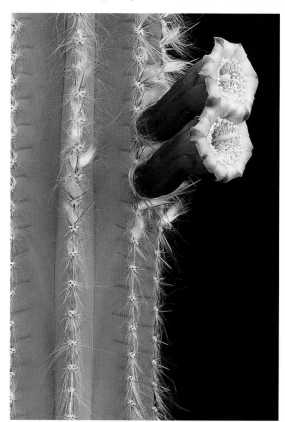

ABOVE Pilosocereus pachycladus *from Brazil has beautiful blue stems, and flowers at night.*

cutting. These rooted top-cuts often start to flower before they have grown much and it is a good way to get a smaller plant that flowers.

PYGMAEOCEREUS BYLESIANUS

This truly dwarf cereoid from the very arid coastal zone of southern Peru is of uncertain affinity but now thought to be related to haageocereus. It forms a small clump of finger-sized stems whilst under the ground and large fleshy roots develop for water storage to keep this tiny plant alive in its harsh environment. It is reasonably easy to cultivate and needs less than average water, although as the clump grows there is tendency for the stems in the middle to dry up. If this happens it is best to break up the clump and start again. It is usually grown from cuttings or splittings from the edge of a clump, which often already have roots. White, nocturnal and sweet-smelling flowers appear spasmodically throughout the summer and are an adaptation for pollination by moths. This very pleasing little plant is rarely offered for sale so you will need to look around to find one.

Coleocephalocereus aureus *will grow a cephalium down one side of the stem for flower production.*

Pygmaeocereus bylesianus *is a miniature plant with sweet-smelling, nocturnal flowers.*

Coleocephalocereus

The Brazilian genus coleocephalocereus has a number of species, many of which live on rock plates in tropical conditions. They grow in leaf litter trapped in depressions or cracks in large rock outcrops such as the famous Sugar Loaf in Rio de Janeiro. In cultivation, they all grow readily from seed and grow best if kept warm and moist.

COLEOCEPHALOCEREUS AUREUS

This species is quite easy to grow if kept in a sunny place and given plenty of water in summer and a minimum temperature of 10°C (50°F) during the winter. The small yellow flowers appear from the cephalium, which is formed on the side of mature stems after about eight years in cultivation. Unlike most of the other species, which have long, trailing stems with their ends turned upwards, this remains more globular, particularly in the form illustrated, known as *C. brevicylindricus*. It can still be found labelled in collections as buiningia, a genus created for this species and *C. purpureus*.
Similar species: *C. purpureus*

Neoraimondia arequipensis from Peru has big felty areoles.

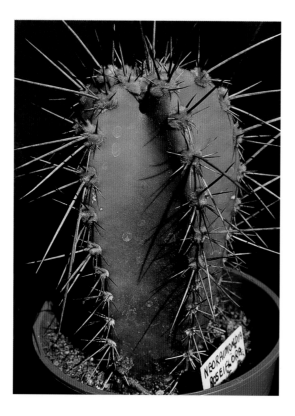

NEORAIMONDIA AREQUIPENSIS

Included here because of its unusual appearance as a seedling, this large-growing species is widespread along the arid coastal zone of Peru where it is the dominant feature of the landscape in some valleys near to the coast. Although very unlikely to flower in cultivation, it is remarkable when it does because each areole is capable of flowering many times and each time it does, it gets longer, so that eventually the areoles become long and peg-shaped. The seedlings, which have long spines and large areoles, are very attractive. Unfortunately, the seed does not always germinate very well and the seedlings are slow growing and susceptible to excess moisture, so careful watering is necessary.

Copiapoa

This well-defined genus has evolved to live in one of the most demanding of habitats, the Atacama desert of northern Chile. In the majority of the distribution zone, rainfall is sparse and infrequent, the plants depending on mists that drift inland from above the cold ocean that is rarely far from where the plants can be found. In some favoured places, copiapoa is the dominant plant, forming magnificent stands of old plants, some of the most spectacular cactus habitats in the world. Others are miniatures, only surviving because of their large tuberous roots, and very difficult to find in habitat. These small species are particularly well suited to cultivation and will grow and flower well in an open compost in good light.

Seeds of many of the less common species are difficult to obtain since the plants often flower irregularly in cultivation, and habitat-collected seed is only available in years of increased rainfall, generally associated with El Niño. In cultivation, the plants should be watered overhead with a fine rose last thing in the evening in summer to simulate the mists that they rely on for moisture in the wild. In this way, the soil gets wetted without being soaked. The small-bodied species will take more water and even in winter a little will stop them dehydrating. A sunny place in the glasshouse with good ventilation suits all the species best. Grafting is sometimes employed to speed the growth of the slowest species but care must be taken not to push them too much otherwise they can grow unnaturally columnar, something they have a tendency to do anyway in culture.

The only complete book in English is *Copiapoa* by Graham Charles, which describes and illustrates all the species. Another good read is *Copiapoa in their Environment* by Rudolf Schulz and Attila Kapitany, which concentrates on the northern species and the places they grow.

Copiapoa cinerea is a choice slow-growing species from Chile.

COPIAPOA CINEREA

This is the most famous species of copiapoa and the one everyone wants in their collection because of its remarkable appearance. In habitat it has a chalky white body with spectacular black spines, but even the most skilled cultivation in a greenhouse can only produce a red-brown body when a seedling, which later turns greyish. Its slow-growing nature adds to its attraction, it can take more than twenty years to get a plant to 10cm (4in) in diameter. Offsets will sometimes form on old plants and these can be used as cuttings for propagation but seed is the usual way to raise more plants. The flowers are yellow and even plants of only 6cm (2.5in) in diameter will occasionally produce blooms. It comes from near Taltal in northern Chile.

Similar species: *C. columna-alba, C. gigantea*

COPIAPOA COQUIMBANA

Found in collections under many names, this is the most widespread species in the wild. It grows from Fray Jorge to Huasco in Chile, the most southerly species of copiapoa. Some forms grow far enough south to benefit from winter rain, which is probably why they are easy to cultivate. Seed is usually available for various forms of this plant and it is straightforward to raise and much quicker growing than *C. cinerea*. It has large yellow flowers and plants of just 6cm (2.5in) in diameter can be expected to bloom from the new areoles in the crown. Some forms

Copiapoa coquimbana *grows slowly but will easily produce its yellow flowers.*

grow naturally elongated bodies while others freely cluster. A deep pot is advisable since it usually has large thickened roots for water storage.

COPIAPOA HUMILIS

One of the small-growing species and the one most frequently seen in collections, this plant grows very easily and flowers when young. It can be recommended to beginners as a good copiapoa to start with, since it can be raised

Copiapoa humilis *is a small, free-flowering species from Chile.*

from seed or by rooting one of the offsets that it freely produces. The clusters can eventually get to 15cm (6in) or more in cultivation and have large, swollen roots for water storage like most of the small species. Large yellow flowers can be expected on plants only 4cm (1.5in) in diameter and a single specimen often produces seed since it is usually self-fertile. It comes from Paposo in northern Chile.

Similar species: *C. tenuissima*

COPIAPOA KRAINZIANA

Probably the most easily recognized species because of its dense covering of glassy white spines, this has always been sought after by col-

Copiapoa krainziana has a dense covering of thin white spines, unique in the genus.

lectors but until recently seed was very rarely available in the trade. Most plants sold by nurseries were rooted offsets from old imported plants. *C. krainziana* forms clusters of stems and the spination varies from very long and soft to short and stiff, depending on the clone. The flowers are yellow but are not freely produced in cultivation. It comes from the hills north of Taltal in northern Chile and was once thought to be very rare but is now known to be plentiful.

COPIAPOA LAUI

Copiapoa laui, the smallest species, slowly making a cluster of stems.

The smallest species in the genus, this was only discovered in the 1970s and was thought at first to be a species of eriosyce. The tiny heads only grow to about 1cm (0.5in) in diameter and offset

to make big mats that are flat to the ground in habitat but form mounds in cultivation. Each head has a thickened taproot, so propagation is easily achieved by removing an offset with its root already formed. Seed is easy to grow but the seedlings are slow for a couple of years. It flowers freely with the usual yellow flowers, and grows easily so long as it is not allowed to get too dry even in winter when an occasional misting will prevent excess shrivelling. It comes from Planta Esmeralda in northern Chile.

Similar species: *C. hypogaea*

Coryphantha

Native to Mexico and the western USA, this genus is related to mammillaria in which its species were included before the erection of coryphantha by Lemaire in 1868. The main differences are the large flowers, which are centrally produced, and the furrow along the top of the tubercles of most species. The closely related escobaria is included here and is similar in appearance and culture to coryphantha. For a number of years these cacti have not been very popular, although most collections include at least a few representatives. Many species of coryphantha look alike and have similar yellow flowers, but there are a few which are more individual or present a challenge in cultivation and some can be slow growing. Similarly, many escobarias look alike with white spines and pale flowers, making the species difficult to identify. A sunny location is essential, with high summer temperatures and a winter minimum of 5°C (41°F) producing the best results. Peat-based soils are not the best choice for the long-term maintenance of these species; they should be grown in Mexican mix (see page 45).

CORYPHANTHA CALIPENSIS

Solitary for many years before clumping sparingly, this species with large tubercles eventually grows to 9cm (3.5in) in height and about 5cm (2in) in diameter. It is similar to many other species with its large yellow flowers appearing throughout the summer from the very woolly centre of the plant. It comes from Puebla, Mexico where it grows on limestone soils.

Similar species: *C. pallida, C. cornifera*

Coryphantha calipensis *has woolly areoles and large yellow flowers.*

ABOVE: Coryphantha elephantidens *usually has pink flowers but they can sometimes be yellow.*

CORYPHANTHA ELEPHANTIDENS

In the best forms the flower of this species is a lovely pink but most clones are more yellow. This is a grassland species and enjoys plenty of water in the summer when it will grow quickly to eventually form a sizeable cluster of stems. The dark, glossy bodies are depressed globular and will produce large flowers when about 10cm (4in) in diameter. It comes from Michoacan, Mexico.

Similar species: *C. bumamma, C. greenwoodii*

CORYPHANTHA RAMILLOSA

Interesting because of its lovely flowers, this small species is only occasionally found in collections but deserves to be better represented. It is solitary for some years but will eventually form a small cluster of slightly elongated stems, each up to 9cm (3.5in) in height. The flowers appear when the plant is only 5cm (2in) in diameter so it is an ideal plant for the collection. It comes from the Big Bend area of Texas, USA where it is said to be scarce.

Coryphantha ramillosa *is unusual in the genus for having pink flowers.*

Escobaria vivipara *ssp.* bisbeeana *can be difficult to grow well.*

Escobaria hesteri – *a miniature gem from Texas, USA.*

BELOW Acharagma roseana *is easily grown and soon makes an impressive clump of stems.*

ESCOBARIA VIVIPARA SSP. BISBEEANA

The extensive distribution area for *E. vivipara* in all its forms extends from Canada down to Texas and across into California. It always presents a challenge in cultivation and good specimens are rarely seen in glasshouses. This subspecies comes from Arizona and nearby Mexico where it forms large clusters in grassland or woodland. The magnificent flowers are easily produced on a plant of only 5cm (2in) in diameter so long as it is given a sunny location.

ESCOBARIA HESTERI

A beautiful dwarf species, very popular in collections for its free-flowering nature and ease of culture. Each body is only about 3cm (1in) in diameter but they cluster to form big clumps. It is one of a number of miniature taxa that come from Brewster County in Texas, USA. The pretty flowers are produced throughout the summer if given adequate watering.

ACHARAGMA ROSEANA

This relatively new generic name will be unfamiliar to many although the plant is well known either as a gymnocactus or an escobaria. The dense yellow spination is the main attraction of this species and it is a shame that the flowers are small and so similar in colour. Very easy to grow, this plant will flower when small and eventually makes large clusters. It comes from Coahuila, Mexico where it grows on steep sandstone hillsides.

Discocactus

This Brazilian genus is included because it is unique, beautiful and a challenge in cultivation. It is not a good choice for a beginner, but after mastering the basics most collectors look for something a bit more difficult. There is certainly a great deal of satisfaction to be found in growing a discocactus to flowering size and enjoying the amazing nocturnal flowers. The mature plant produces a cephalium in the growing point consisting of wool and bristles

A group of young discocacti of various species showing their ability to flower synchronously.

from where the flowers will emerge. After this happens, the plant body will continue to grow – some species are capable of growing to over 25cm (10in) in diameter, even though flowering may have commenced at less than half that size. Although the cephalium is a structure produced especially for flowering, it may also protect the young buds, which, once visible, grow very quickly, and in warm weather a plant may bloom the next night. The flowers are white and strongly scented, ideal for pollination by hawk moths, which have long tongues to reach the nectary at the base of the flower tube.

It is remarkable how discocacti are able to synchronize their flowering to maximize pollination. Even in cultivation, large numbers of plants, which may be of different species, will flower together then many nights will pass with hardly any flowers. The stimulus for this behaviour is unknown, but atmospheric pressure, phases of the moon and temperature have all been suggested.

The key requirement for successful culture is heat, a warm and sunny place in summer and a minimum temperature of 15°C (59°F) in winter. They need an open, acidic soil, so the standard mix with extra grit is suitable (see page 45). A popular approach is to graft discocactus seedlings on echinopsis, which certainly makes cultivation

much easier, reducing the risk of the plant rotting, which tends to be the greatest problem.

A well-illustrated reference book about this fascinating genus is *Discocactus* by Albert Buining.

DISCOCACTUS PLACENTIFORMIS

One of the most widespread species from Minas Gerais, Brazil, this plant grows a solitary body up to 30cm (12in) in diameter. In some places it can be found growing under trees in sand whilst in others it will be in the open on rock plates. The flowers are up to 7cm (2.75in) in length and usually occur in clusters, filling the air with sweet perfume. It must be raised from seeds, which are large and need to be sown within a year of harvesting to get good germination. It will grow quickly so long as it is kept really warm and moist.

Similar species: *D. heptacanthus, D. bahiensis*

DISCOCACTUS HORSTII

The smallest solitary species and the most individual, this plant is one of the most sought after of all cacti. It is difficult to grow on its own roots

Discocactus placentiformis *from Brazil has large nocturnal flowers pollinated by moths.*

Discocactus horstii, *a small species with unusual spines and sweet-smelling, nocturnal flowers.*

and the best results are obtained by grafting it on a small stock, which can then be buried. Raising it from seed requires great skill and patience although heat is the key to success. In its natural home in Minas Gerais, Brazil, it grows in quartz gravel where its survival has been threatened by the mining of the crystals. The spine clusters are unlike any others and its dark body, spectacular flowers and difficulty of cultivation will always attract the keen collector.

Echinocactus

This very old name was applied to a broad range of globular cacti in the nineteenth century before most were transferred into newly created genera, so leaving echinocactus with just a few species. The similar and larger genus ferocactus is included here since they are similar from a cultivator's point of view. These plants are generally large growing, cultivated for their spination and architectural impact rather than their flowers, which are not easily produced in small greenhouses.

The most commonly grown large globular cactus is probably *Echinocactus grusonii*, the golden barrel, a spectacular plant which looks its best when used outdoors in a suitable climate such as the Mediterranean.

Ferocacti are also effective in outdoor bedding schemes, their spines being brightly coloured, especially the reds, which are particularly intense when wet. They come from Mexico and the south-west USA and some can grow into spectacular clumps of immense size. A few species are smaller and can be persuaded to flower in a 15cm (6in) pot if given a bright situation. None is difficult to grow but plenty of root room with maximum light and heat in summer produces the best specimens. Closely related to ferocactus is leuchtenbergia with its curious long tubercles.

ECHINOCACTUS GRUSONII 'GOLDEN BARREL'

One of the most familiar cacti in cultivation, this fast-growing species is one of the best for golden spines and is the easiest large-growing globular cactus to cultivate. It is extensively used for outdoor landscaping, producing yellow flowers when about 40cm (16in) in diameter, depend-

Echinocactus grusonii *will grow large before producing its yellow flowers.*

ing on the amount of sun it receives. The stem remains solitary for many years but it will eventually form clusters. Although it is extremely common in cultivation, it is rare in its Mexican home, especially since a recently constructed dam flooded part of its limited habitat. There are some cultivars available, one with white spines and another that is almost spineless, but neither is an improvement on the original.

Similar species: *E. platyacanthus*

FEROCACTUS GRACILIS SSP COLORATUS

The majority of species in this genus are very large growing and most collections will only have room for a few. They are well suited to outdoor plantings in suitably sunny and warm climates where the beauty of the spines will be fully developed. Most are solitary, only a few will form clusters with age. For glasshouse culture there are some that will flower at a reasonable size such as *F. macrodiscus*, *F. glaucescens*, *F. hamatacanthus* and *F. schwarzii* but these are not the best spined in the genus. Most are easy to grow but need a sunny place to look their best. They come from Mexico and the USA and some become very large; the tallest of all is *F. diguetii* from the island of Santa Catalina off the coast of Baja, which grows up to 4m (13ft) in height.

A large group of mature Echinocactus grusonii *at the Huntington Botanical Gardens, California.*

Ferocactus macrodiscus *will flower in a small pot in a glasshouse.*

LEUCHTENBERGIA PRINCIPIS

This is a very distinct species because of its long tubercles, unlike those on any other cactus. The large yellow flowers are reminiscent of ferocactus to which this plant is related. It will eventually grow to 50cm (19.5in) in height when it will form a woody trunk and sometimes branch. Its habitat range is a large area of north and

Ferocactus gracilis *ssp.* coloratus *is a large barrel cactus with colourful spines.*

central Mexico, but individuals are widespread and plants are rarely found in large numbers at any one location. It is easy to grow from seed in a sunny spot with plenty of water in the summer and a good-sized pot. Flowering can be expected when the plant is in a 12cm (5in) pot.

Leuchtenbergia principis *is unique because of its extremely long tubercles.*

Echinocereus

A popular subject for a specialist collection, echinocerei are known to have some of the most beautiful flowers of all cacti. Native to Mexico and the south-west USA, the genus includes large as well as miniature species. Another once separate genus, wilcoxia, which has thin stems and tuberous roots, is now included in echinocereus.

Most species are easy to grow in a bright location, some being very hardy and capable of withstanding frost while others are quite tender, depending on their natural environment. A frequently encountered characteristic of the flowers is the colour of the stigma lobes, which are usually, but not always, green. The flower buds often burst through the epidermis, so after flowering a prominent scar is left behind. This is uncommon in cacti but copiapoa, for example, also do a similar thing.

There have been a number of good reference books about the genus published in recent years: *Echinocereus* by N.P.Taylor was the foundation of today's classification; *Echinocereus* edited by Lino Di Martino is a good picture book; and *Echinocereus* by Blum et al is the most recent complete handbook.

Echinocereus engelmannii *has beautiful flowers and enjoys sunshine.*

ECHINOCEREUS ENGELMANNII

This species, commonly found in the south-west of the USA, makes large clumps of elongated stems with strong spines of various colours. Given a sunny place in a glasshouse, it will grow quickly and produce its magnificent flowers from the side of the stem just as it starts to cluster at about five years of age. It is easily grown from seed, which is the usual method of propagation. The spines make this plant attractive even when not in flower.

Similar species: *E. fendleri, E. fasciculatus, E. brandegeei*

ECHINOCEREUS NIVOSUS

One of the few white-spined echinocerei, this is easily grown and freely produces its red flowers that contrast beautifully with the stems. Even as a young plant it will begin to offset and in time makes a large clump of stems each up to12cm (5in) in length. Given a sunny locality it will have a good crop of flowers, which are borne from areoles on the sides of the stems. Its natural habitat is in Coahuila, Mexico.

Similar species: *E. laui*

ECHINOCEREUS LONGISETUS SSP. DELAETII

Here is a very individual looking species with long white hairs reminiscent of an espostoa. It needs a very bright locality to grow well, soon

Echinocereus nivosus *is one of the best white-spined species.*

Echinocereus rigidissimus *ssp.* rubrispinus *has eye-catching red spines and splendid flowers.*

Echinocereus longisetus *ssp.* delaetii *is unique in the genus for its long white hair.*

making a clump of thick stems which then might produce its lovely pink flowers but only sparingly. Less than average water at all times suits this choice plant that is best raised from seed. It comes from Coahuila, Mexico.

ECHINOCEREUS PECTINATUS

Echinocereus pectinatus *is prized for its wonderfully coloured pectinate spines.*

One of a number of pectinate-spined echinocerei that are very popular with collectors because of their attractive stems and spectacular flowers. It should be said that these species are not easy to tell apart and are frequently wrongly labelled. All enjoy as much sun as possible and less than average water. They are prone to growth rings and creasing of the body,

often due to root loss. When grown well they are impressive plants and do occasionally cluster. This one originates from northern Mexico.

Similar species: *E. rigidissimus, E. dasyacanthus, E. reichenbachii*

ECHINOCEREUS RUSSANTHUS

This is one of a few species of echinocereus that have small green or brown flowers and are difficult to distinguish. All forms grow and flower easily and are very tolerant of low temperatures in winter. Easily raised from seed, most form clusters of short stems with attractive spination from which the small flowers are often borne in large numbers. They come from Texas and New Mexico, USA.

Similar species: *E. chloranthus, E. viridiflorus*

ECHINOCEREUS SUBINERMIS

Probably the best of the yellow-flowered echinocerei, this species gives no problems in cultivation and easily produces its large showy flowers. The stems only have a few ribs and hardly any spines, which gives it a very individual appearance. It is usually raised from seed although the offsets root without difficulty. There is a spinier form called *E. subinermis* ssp. *ochoterenae*. Both come from Northern Mexico.

Similar species: *E. stoloniferus*

Echinocereus pulchellus *is a miniature plant with neat spines and pretty flowers.*

BELOW: Echinocereus knippelianus *is very popular in competitions and shows.*

ABOVE Echinocereus russanthus *has unusual green or brownish flowers.*

Echinocereus subinermis *has the biggest yellow flowers in the genus.*

ECHINOCEREUS PULCHELLUS

Among the smallest of the genus, this plant grows a solitary stem close to the ground, retreating under the soil in dry times, and has an enlarged root for water storage. A very popular miniature, it is normally raised from seed and produces its pretty pink flowers when only a few centimetres across. Native to Hidalgo, Mexico, it grows in grassland where it is threatened by agricultural development.

Similar species: *E. pulchellus* ssp. *weinbergii*

ECHINOCEREUS KNIPPELIANUS

Perhaps the most popular plant in the genus, this naturally solitary species can make quite large clusters in cultivation. There are a number of forms, some of which produce their flowers from the centre of the plant, which is unusual in echinocereus, and these forms are normally more caespitose. Care should be taken not to damage the swollen root since it is prone to rot, and less than average water will retain the natural appearance of the stem and avoid it splitting, which can happen if over-watered. Another species from Mexico, it can readily be raised from seed.

ECHINOCEREUS SCHMOLLII

Once belonging to the genus wilcoxia, this plant is very different from the other species of echinocereus described here. It has thin, branching stems covered in fine hairs that grow from a large underground tuber evolved for water storage. The pretty pink flowers, which are like those of other echinocerei, grow from near the tips of the stems. In cultivation, the stems can be rather lax and should occasionally be pruned to encourage new growth. The severed pieces can be used as cuttings or new plants can be grown from seed. It is known in only a few localities in southern Mexico and is considered endangered.

Echinocereus schmollii *has thin hairy stems and a big underground root.*

Echinopsis

This large genus from South America includes both small species with beautiful flowers and some of the largest columnar cacti (formerly of the genus trichocereus). The latter are not described here since they are largely unsuitable for greenhouse culture except as grafting stocks for less robust species (see page 59).

The desirable, small, day-flowering species were formerly classified in the genus lobivia, which is still the name usually found on their labels today. They are very easy to cultivate and most can survive sub-zero temperatures so long as they are kept dry in winter. The flowers are especially attractive with red, pink, purple, orange, yellow and white all represented. Individuals with different flower colours may be found in the same population in the wild, and it is possible to get various colours from a batch of seed, so it is worth keeping a few plants until they flower.

Echinopsis in the strict sense has long, tubular flowers that are usually white and often flower at night. It has been extensively hybridized to perfect the flowers and extend the flowering period (see page 33).

The only references for lobivias are found in the work of Walter Rausch, the leading exponent of the genus in recent years. His most recent publication *Lobivia 85* is in German but an earlier work *Lobivia* is available in an English translation.

ECHINOPSIS GLAUCINA

The plant will be familiar even if the name used here is not. The beautiful glaucous blue body belongs to the plant long known as *Acanthocalycium glaucum*, a native of an arid part of north-west Argentina. It is easy to cultivate in a sunny spot in the greenhouse, and produces its large yellow flowers from areoles on the shoulder of the plant when only 8cm (3in) in diameter. It must be grown from seed, which presents no difficulty although the blueness of the body varies from individual to individual. When fully grown it may become slightly columnar, but the stem remains solitary.

Similar species: *E. thionantha*

Echinopsis glaucina *has a glaucous blue body and spectacular yellow flowers.*

ECHINOPSIS SPINIFLORA

Better known as *Acanthocalycium violaceum*, this is a variable species from Cordoba in central-west Argentina. The violet flower of this form is unusual in the family *Cactaceae*, making it a popular plant to cultivate. There are forms with white flowers and the yellow spination can be sparse or more dense and long. The solitary, bright green body can grow to over 15cm (6in) in diameter, although it flowers from the crown when only 8cm (3in). It appreciates plenty of water in the summer and is very easy to grow from seed.

Echinopsis spiniflora, *an Argentinian plant with unusual violet flowers.*

ECHINOPSIS MARSONERI

The spectacular black-throated flowers are the main attraction of this species that has long been known as a lobivia. The stems cluster to form a small group that in habitat is almost buried, particularly in the dry season when the heads are flush with the ground and difficult to see. There are many flower colour variants including yellow, red and orange for which many names have been used. *E. marsoneri* grows in northern Argentina, high in the mountains where it can be very cold, so it will survive frost in cultivation if kept dry. The large roots store water to help it survive the long dry winters. Propagation is by seeds or cuttings, which are easily rooted.

Echinopsis marsoneri *has beautiful flowers with a dark throat.*

ECHINOPSIS PENTLANDII

Known to collectors for many years, this former lobivia is very variable in spination as well as flower size and colour. Flowers can be up to 7cm (2.75in) in diameter and colours range from white, through shades of yellow to pink, lilac and red. Many of these forms have been given names as often happens with variable plants, but the similarity in the form of the flowers shows their close relationship. *E. pentlandii* may be found in Peru and Bolivia where it makes large clusters of spiny stems in its high-altitude home. There is no problem with cold so long as it is kept dry in the winter. Growing from seed is straightforward, as is propagation by rooting offsets.

Similar species: *E. maximiliana*

Echinopsis pentlandii *can have flowers of various colours.*

Echinopsis ferox *can grow large with long, dense spination.*

ECHINOPSIS TIEGELIANA

An example of one of the smaller clustering species that were once in the genus lobivia, this free-flowering plant is easy to grow – ideal for the beginner. It is undemanding in cultivation, quickly making large clusters of neatly spined miniature stems. The relatively large flowers are easily produced and can be yellow or shades of red. It is normally propagated from offsets, which can be rooted in the usual way. It comes from Bolivia and northern Argentina where it grows in places with reliable summer rainfall.

Similar species: *E. arachnacantha*

ECHINOPSIS FEROX

Echinopsis tiegeliana *is a small species with yellow or red flowers.*

The extensive habitat of this majestic plant stretches from Argentina to Bolivia. The large solitary stems can become football-sized with

long, dense spination and whilst some populations only grow to the size of an orange, in the north of the range they become columnar up to 1m (3ft) in height. Most forms have white flowers, but those near the border can have flowers ranging in colour from lilac to red and were known as *Lobivia longispina*. They are easy to grow but some forms need to be at least 12cm (5in) in diameter before producing long-tubed, spectacular flowers in the spring.

Similar species: *E. aurea*

ECHINOPSIS HAEMATANTHA

This small-growing species, formerly known as a lobivia, comes from the mountains of northern Argentina where it can be difficult to find, particularly after the long dry period in winter. It has thickened roots like many cacti from that region and produces its spectacular flowers after the first rains in spring. It is not as easy to cultivate as most echinopsis and care must be taken not to let it stay wet for too long, so less than average water and a sunny place in the

Echinopsis haematantha, *a miniature plant from the Andes with various flower colours.*

Echinopsis huascha *makes big clumps of elongated stems.*

glasshouse are recommended. Offsets are not usually produced, so seed is the best method of propagation. The seedlings will flower when about 3cm (1in) in diameter.

ECHINOPSIS HUASCHA

Easy to distinguish from other echinopsis because of its elongated stems that can make very large clumps. Its short-tubed flowers come in a variety of colours from yellow to red, which can appear on plants growing together in habitat. Native to north-west Argentina, near to the town of Chiliceto it makes hybrids with another echinopsis, which produces a fantastic range of flower colours. Easy and quick to grow from seed, this plant needs a good-sized pot to enable it to reach its potential. Plenty of water in summer and a sunny spot will result in strong spines and eventually many lovely flowers.

ECHINOPSIS BRUCHII

Among the largest of the globular cacti, this is one of a number of species that were placed in the genus soehrensia, all of which make large heads up to 1m (3ft) in diameter and up to 2m (6.5ft) in height, often clustering to make huge mounds. The spination of this plant is quite open compared to the similar species *E. formosa*, which is covered in long, dense spines. It grows quickly if given enough root space,

BELOW Echinopsis bruchii *is one of the biggest species from the high Andes.*

plenty of water and a sunny position in the summer, but it can take some time before flowering as it usually needs to be at least 20cm (8in) in diameter.

Similar species: *E. formosa*

ECHINOPSIS EYRIESII

The 'classic' echinopsis, this must have been cultivated on more window-sills than any other cactus. The copious offsets are so easy to root and the plant so easy to grow that the same few clones must have been in cultivation for years. They look much like the drawings from the early nineteenth century when the plant was described. Unfortunately, these clones are not reliable at flowering so this beautiful species from Uruguay and southern Brazil has a reputation for being difficult to flower, which is not the case if you grow a good clone. The flowers, which are often perfumed, can be white or pale lilac and are nocturnal but usually stay open the following morning. The bright green bodies grow to 12cm (5in) in diameter but will flower at half that size. It is a good idea to remove most of the many offsets, leaving the main head to grow into a good-looking specimen.

Similar species: *E. albispinosa, E. huotii*

Echinopsis ancistrophora, *a small species with long-tubed white flowers.*

ECHINOPSIS ANCISTROPHORA

A widespread, small-growing species with the typical long-tubed echinopsis flowers. It grows in damp places in Argentina and Bolivia, often among grass, and enjoys plenty of water in the summer. Very easy to grow and flower, it only needs to be 4cm (1.5in) in diameter before it produces spectacular white blooms that dwarf the plant. Some forms become larger with stronger spinization but they are all similarly easy and rewarding to cultivate.

ECHINOPSIS RHODACANTHA SSP. CHACOANA

This is one of a group of echinopsis with long-tubed white flowers, but a different internal structure and brown tubes. The most commonly seen example is the widespread *E. leucantha*, which occurs over a large part of western Argentina and can grow to 1m (3ft) in height. *E. rhodacantha* ssp. *chacoana* comes from the

Echinopsis eyriesii *has pink or white nocturnal flowers.*

Echinopsis rhodacantha *ssp.* chacoana *grows under shrubs in the Paraguayan Chaco.*

a huge choice of colours. Hylocereus and selenicereus have long branches that root along their length and can become very large thickets – their flowers are among the largest of all cacti. Less often cultivated are the varied species of rhipsalis with jointed stems, which can be cylindrical, flat or angled, sometimes mixed on one plant. The flowers are small but often produced in large

Disocactus flagelliformis *is an ideal plant for a hanging basket.*

Chaco of Paraguay where it grows under the dense shrubs that cover this hot and arid area. It is not difficult to cultivate and will flower when about 8cm (3in) in diameter, the buds often appearing from areoles well down the sides of the stem.

Similar species: *E. leucantha*

Epiphytic Cacti

These plants are quite unlike other cacti since they have adapted to life among the trees of tropical forests rather than the semi-arid localities favoured by most others. Although some can have roots in the ground, most grow in leaf litter on the branches of trees or over rocks.

The best known epiphytic cacti belong to the genus epiphyllum – large and beautiful flowers are produced from the leaf-like stems of these plants, which have been extensively hybridized, resulting in spectacular flowers in

ABOVE: *Schlumbergera hybrids brighten the days of winter with their variously coloured flowers.* Photo: John Pilbeam

RIGHT: Disocactus macranthus *from Mexico has small, exotic flowers.* Photo: John Pilbeam

BELOW: Lepismium houlletiana *enjoys a warm and shady environment.* Photo: Bill Weightman

numbers and are followed by small fruits, hence the common name 'mistletoe cactus' for ones with white berries. Popular for window-sill culture are the so-called 'Christmas' and 'Easter' cacti, their flat-jointed stems terminating in colourful flowers around the appropriate season.

All these plants grow best in a warm, shady environment with constant moisture in the summer and a little in winter, when a minimum temperature of 5°C (41°F) is adequate for most species. The soil should have plenty of humus so extra peat, peat substitute or leaf mould should be added to the standard mix (see page 45).

Many epiphytes, especially disocactus and rhipsalis, are well suited to growing in a hanging basket, but it should be hung under shaded glass unless the greenhouse is situated in a naturally shady place. Selenicereus and hylocereus benefit from a large pot or a free root run where they will quickly grow and produce their huge, sweet-smelling, nocturnal flowers. They can be trained into the roof of the glasshouse to great effect.

All epiphytic cacti can be easily propagated from cuttings that are simple to root if given warm, damp conditions.

A recent book about schlumbergera and hybrids is *Christmas Cacti* by A.J.S. McMillan

Hatiora salicornioides *makes a good houseplant and flowers freely.* Photo: John Pilbeam

Epiphyllum hybrids like 'Beauty' are available in a huge range of colours and shapes.

BELOW: Epiphyllum *'Pegasus'*. Photo: John Pilbeam

Hylocereus polyrhizus *has large nocturnal flowers with a strong perfume.*

and J.F. Horobin; The Rainbow Gardens catalogue *Jungle Cacti* has many descriptions and good pictures; and *Epiphyllum* by M. Leue is well illustrated with excellent photographs.

Eriosyce

This genus was originally erected in the nineteenth century for a widespread, large-growing plant from the Chilean Andes, *E. aurata*. A number of further genera: neoporteria; horridocactus; neochilenia; pyrrhocactus; islaya and thelocephala were subsequently created for other related plants from Chile, Peru and Argentina. These have all recently been united under the genus eriosyce although the former generic names are still often used.

Eriosyce now includes a diverse assortment of plants from the cultivator's point of view. Some are very large growing while others are miniatures, the flower form varies depending on the pollinator and the fruits also exhibit a wide variation. Although some species are easy to grow, such as those originally in the genus neoporteria, others are a real challenge – *E. (Pyrrhocactus) umadeave* from Argentina is one of the most difficult of all cacti to cultivate.

Because their habitats are often very arid, perhaps only receiving moisture from incoming sea mists rather than actual rainfall, some have developed tuberous roots for the storage of water; these roots sometimes being larger than the body of the plant above ground. Tuberous-rooted species are especially susceptible to rotting if over-watered, and a well-drained, principally mineral soil is the best medium for these and indeed all the genus.

The most complete book on the genus is *Eriosyce* by Fred Kattermann.

Eriosyce senilis *can have white, yellow or brown spines.*

Eriosyce napina ssp. lembckei *is a free-flowering miniature plant from Chile.*

ERIOSYCE SENILIS

This densely spined plant belongs to the group of species formerly known as neoporterias that have tubular flowers evolved for pollination by humming-birds. They are easy to grow in a glasshouse in Europe if given a bright, well-ventilated locality. The stem remains solitary and will flower when only 6cm (2.5in) in diameter. This species can be found with white, yellow or dark brown spines, all colours growing together on the steep hillsides near the coast of northern Chile.

ERIOSYCE NAPINA SSP. LEMBCKEI

A few species of eriosyce have small bodies and large swollen roots. They were once included in the genus thelocephala and all have very bristly flower tubes. Their bodies grow almost level with the ground or beneath it in dry periods, and are difficult to find in their Chilean habitat. Much prized by collectors for their small size and neat spination, they are slow but not difficult to grow, and will flower when quite small, just a few centimetres in diameter. Less than average water and a sunny spot are the ingredients for successful cultivation.

Similar species: *E. esmeraldana, E. krausii, E. odieri*

ERIOSYCE ISLAYENSIS

One of a distinctive group of eriosyce once known as the genus islaya, this species is mainly to be found in southern Peru rather than Chile, where it may now be extinct due to increased aridity in the area. These plants are mainly dependent on mists moving in from above the cold sea for moisture rather than rainfall, which rarely occurs. In cultivation they are grown from seed and require a sunny place with less than average water that is best applied overhead with a fine rose in the evening. The easily produced flowers, which are usually yellow, rarely pink and sometimes very small, are followed by large, pink sack-like fruits that disperse the seeds in nature by being blown across the ground.

Similar species: *E. omasensis*

ERIOSYCE BULBOCALYX

There are a few species of eriosyce that come from Argentina and formerly belonged to the genus pyrrhocactus. They are more of a challenge in cultivation than the ones from Chile, but this plant will grow and flower in a sunny spot. Care must be taken with watering, which should only be done in warm weather. The flowers are urn-shaped, which is unusual in the genus, and as the solitary stem matures it will grow long, upward-pointing curved spines, giving it a distinctive appearance. Seed is occasionally available but germination is not usually good.

Similar species: *E. umadeave, E. megliolii, E. villicumensis*

Eriosyce islayensis *comes from the dry coastal desert of southern Peru.*

Eriosyce bulbocalyx *has curious, urn-shaped flowers.*

Eriosyce strausiana *from Argentina is rarely seen in cultivation.*

ERIOSYCE STRAUSIANA

Another of the Argentinian species, this is widespread in the wild but rarely cultivated, perhaps because the seed is rarely available. The solitary body often has a brownish epidermis and tends to grow slightly columnar with age. The flowers appear from the crown when the plant is over 5cm (2in) in diameter and are usually yellow, but in the form illustrated (*E. andreaeana*) they are more red in appearance. A sunny location and average water suits this plant in cultivation.

ERIOSYCE HEINRICHIANA SSP. INTERMEDIA

BELOW: Eriosyce heinrichiana *ssp.* intermedia *produces its pretty flowers even when still small.*

BOTTOM: Eriosyce occulta *from Chile has an attractive dark brown body.*

There are many small-growing, usually solitary, dark-bodied species from Chile that have a normal bee-pollinated flower followed by a fleshy fruit, which falls off whole and leaves a basal pore through which the loose seeds can fall. Once called neochilenias or sometimes pyrrhocactus, these rewarding plants are easy to grow and never take up much space in the glasshouse, although they will grow larger in culture than in their harsh natural environment. The flowers are pink, white or yellow and are easy to raise from seed.

Similar species: *E. napina, E. occulta, E. crispa*

Eriosyce simulans *looks a lot like the copiapoas that grow alongside it.*

ERIOSYCE SIMULANS

Larger growing than *E. heinrichiana* ssp. *intermedia*, this species will form a solitary body up to 15cm (6in) tall, but will produce its pretty flowers from the new areoles when only half that size. It is called 'simulans' because it looks so much like *Copiapoa coquimbana* that grows with it in its natural habitat. In fact, they look so alike that they are difficult to tell apart when out of flower. There is no problem raising this plant from seed and it has no special cultural requirements.

ERIOSYCE TALTALENSIS SSP. ECHINUS

You can find this plant hiding among the rocks in the dry coastal valleys of northern Chile. It can have a splendid covering of fine white hairs that envelop the bluish body, although the extent of this feature varies between individuals. The best forms are known as 'floccosus' and when they flower, the pink petals contrast very

Eriosyce taltalensis ssp. echinus *can have a dense covering of wool over the body.*

well with the white hair. Easy to grow from seed in a bright place, the slightly elongated body will flower when about 6cm (2.5in) in diameter.

Similar species: *E. taltalensis* ssp. *paucicostata*

ERIOSYCE CURVISPINUS

This species grows in the winter rainfall area of Chile as far south as the capital, Santiago. Once known as horridocactus, it is renowned for being difficult to cultivate, but will grow and flower well if watered early in the year and kept almost dry in the height of summer with just a little water again in autumn. It is a winter grower like some other succulents and retains that rhythm in cultivation. The flat, solitary body can become large but the pastel-shaded flowers first appear when the plant is only 8cm (3in) or so in diameter.

Similar species: *E. engleri, E. garavantae, E. limariensis*

Eriosyce curvispinus is rarely seen in collections, *as it is difficult to grow.*

Gymnocalycium

This large genus from South America is very popular with enthusiasts and often the subject of a specialist collection. The species are difficult to differentiate for the beginner, and indeed for the more experienced collector. The classification is largely based upon the appearance of the seeds, which broadly supports five groupings, an approach that is borne out by the geographic distribution. Plants occur naturally over a vast area of Argentina, Bolivia, Uruguay, Paraguay and southern Brazil, with a variety of habitat preferences but rarely in fully exposed arid environments.

In cultivation most are easy to grow, tolerating some shade and enjoying regular moisture in the growing season. Like many South American cacti, they are sensitive to alkalinity and will quickly lose their roots if the soil is not kept slightly acidic (see page 45). Most species have whitish flowers but a few are red, pink or yellow and these are particularly popular.

The best reference book in English is *Gymnocalycium, A Collector's Guide* by John Pilbeam. For the enthusiastic specialist, there is a very active group in Austria called Gymnocalycium.

The various forms of Gymnocalycium bruchii *make a colourful sight in early spring.*

Gymnocalycium monvillei *can have pink or white flowers.*

GYMNOCALYCIUM MONVILLEI

This species, discovered long ago in the mountains just to the west of Cordoba in central Argentina, is better known under the name *G. multiflorum*. It has wonderful golden spines and individual heads can reach a diameter of 15cm (6in), sometimes making big clusters. The flowers are produced on heads about 10cm (4in) across and are white or pale lilac. It is very easy to grow from seed and soon makes an impressive specimen if given plenty of water in the summer.

Similar species: *G. monvillei* ssp. *achirasense*, *G. monvillei* ssp. *horridispinum*

GYMNOCALYCIUM PFLANZII

A large-growing species that has been given many names because of its extensive habitat and variable appearance. It comes from Bolivia and northern Argentina where it usually grows under bushes. The individual heads can grow to over 30cm (12in) in diameter, making it one of the largest species of gymnocalycium, and some forms are freely clustering. The flowers are borne near the crown of the plant and are usually white with a pink throat, but some forms are an unusual apricot or pink. The seeds are small so the seedlings grow slowly at first but soon speed up. It is easy to grow if given plenty of water in the summer, and will flower when about 8cm (3in) or so in diameter.

Similar species: *G. saglionis*

Gymnocalycium pflanzii *is a large species with red-throated flowers.*

GYMNOCALYCIUM HOSSEI

Although an unfamiliar name, many well-known plants from Argentina are now included in this species. They are all densely spined, generally solitary and have the white flower with a red throat common to many gymnocalyciums. *G. hossei* is easy to raise from seed and soon grows an impressive spination if given a sunny position in the greenhouse. The flowers first appear from the new areoles after about four years. Many other species look like this plant and mis-identification of the group is common.

Similar species: *G. castellanosii*, *G. catamarcense*, *G. ritterianum*

Gymnocalycium hossei *from Argentina is covered with strong spines.*

GYMNOCALYCIUM SPEGAZZINII

Here we have one of the best of the entire genus for the collector and exhibitor. It is slow growing, eventually making a very neatly spined, flat-globose, solitary stem up to 15cm (6in) in diameter. It is widespread at high altitude in the north of Argentina and the spination can be short and sparse or long and dense, depending on where the seed originally came from. Given a bright situation, the pale pink flowers are produced sporadically from the centre over a long period in the summer. When grown from seed, it will flower when about five years old and 6cm (2.5in) in diameter.

Similar species: *G. spegazzinii* ssp. *cardenasianum*, *G. bayrianum*

GYMNOCALYCIUM RIOJENSE

Another good species for the show exhibitor because of its slow growth – the solitary brown body will grow up to 10cm (4in) in diameter but it can take twenty years of culture to do so.

Gymnocalycium riojense, *one of the slowest-growing species.*

However, the pink flowers are produced from the crown on much younger plants when only 5cm (2in) in diameter. This is one of a number of similar species that grow in flat ground or on gentle slopes, often under bushes, in northern Argentina. Even though it is slow, it is not difficult to grow and will tolerate light shade.

Similar species: *G. bodenbenderianum*, *G. ochoterenae*, *G. ragonesii*, *G. stellatum*

GYMNOCALYCIUM MIHANOVICHII

This is a very individual type of gymnocalycium from Paraguay and northern Argentina where it grows under bushes in the hot lowland called the Chaco. The unusual flowers can be green, yellowish or white and are produced from the new areoles at the crown of the small, solitary plant. A well-grown specimen will always be highly regarded at a show because it is more difficult to cultivate than most other species of the genus. It requires more warmth in winter when it should be lightly watered on bright days. In the summer it needs some shade and steady moisture. It was from plants like this that the red variegated form 'Ruby Ball' was selected (see page 37).

Similar species: *G. stenopleurum*, *G. anisitsii*

Gymnocalycium spegazzinii *is a slow-growing, choice species from high altitude.*

Gymnocalycium mihanovichii *needs to be kept warm in winter for best results.*

Gymnocalycium bruchii, *a dwarf, early-flowering species ideal for the beginner.*

GYMNOCALYCIUM DELAETII

The northernmost relative of the widespread *G. schickendantzii*, this species grows under bushes in northern Argentina. The flowers are produced in succession in a ring around the waist of the plant in a way not seen in any other species, and have long tubes with either white or pink petals. The solitary stem can get large, up to 25cm (10in) in diameter, and has a brownish epidermis. It grows easily from seed if given plenty of water in the summer and will flower when about 10cm (4in) in diameter.

Similar species: *G. schickendantzii, G. marsoneri*

Gymnocalycium delaetii *has unusual flowers borne around the side of the plant.*

Gymnocalycium andreae *is the best of the yellow-flowering species.*

GYMNOCALYCIUM BRUCHII

An ideal beginner's plant, this is one of the smallest gymnocalyciums and is easy to grow into a large cluster of heads. Available in a wide variety of body sizes and spine colours, the densely white-spined forms are among the most attractive. They all grow in the mountains to the west of Cordoba in central Argentina, where they can be found in shallow soils in grassland. The flowers appear early in the year on many of the small heads in a clump and can be white or pink. The similar *G. andreae* usually has striking yellow flowers. Propagation is achieved either from seed or by removing one of the many offsets that are formed around the main head and often already have roots.

Similar species: *G. andreae, G. calochlorum, G. taningaense, G. parvulum*

Gymnocalycium baldianum *produces its bright red flowers on small plants.*

Gymnocalycium buenekeri *is a Brazilian species with pink flowers.*

GYMNOCALYCIUM BALDIANUM

Here is a species that grows at high altitude, often in countryside that looks like moorland, in the mountains of Argentina around Catamarca. The rich organic soils and plentiful rainfall of its homeland give the clues to its successful cultivation. Plenty of water in the summer and some light shade will be rewarded with a healthy floriferous plant. It is one of the best red flowering species and can be grown from seed to flowering in just three years. It has been used in the production of hybrids that have a wide range of flower colours.

GYMNOCALYCIUM BUENEKERI

A very popular species with collectors, this distinctive plant grows quickly to make clusters of stems that usually have just five ribs. It needs plenty of water in the summer and a generously sized pot, as it will soon become a large specimen. The flowers, which are produced a few at a time, are large and can be various shades of pink – a lovely dark pink in the best clones. Coming from southern Brazil, it grows in deep soils where much of the body can be buried, which makes it difficult to find, and it is now reported as rare in its few known localities. This easily grown species is usually propagated from offsets since the seeds can be difficult to set in cultivation, perhaps because each plant is usually either male or female, a phenomenon found in a number of gymnocalycium species.
    Similar species: *G. horstii*, *G. denudatum*, *G. paraguayense*

GYMNOCALYCIUM NETRELIANUM

Widespread in Uruguay and southern Brazil, this is a yellow-flowered species that can occasionally be found with pink flowers in some populations. It is another example of a species where most individuals are either male or female. Easy to grow from seed or rooted offsets, this rewarding plant will flower when only 5cm (2in) in diameter and in some forms the main head can grow to 10cm (4in). It should be kept moist in summer in a lightly shaded place.
    Similar species: *G. rauschii*

Gymnocalycium netrelianum *is one of the few species with yellow flowers.*

Mammillaria

Often the subject of a specialist collection, the genus mammillaria includes around 300 species. There is remarkable diversity within the genus that includes a pleasing mixture of sizes, shapes and spine colours. A few species remain solitary, but most form clusters of stems that may grow into large clumps, while many of the most popular types are slow growing and remain manageable even in the smallest glasshouse. There are many attractive, white-spined species, which add brightness to a collection and are often seen on the show bench, probably because they are said to appeal to the judges.

Unlike most cacti, which have ribs, mammillarias have tubercles which, like ribs, allow the body to expand and contract depending on the water content. Another unusual feature is that the flowers are produced from the axils rather than from the tip of the tubercles where the spines grow. These flowers often occur in large numbers and make a ring around the crown of the plant, usually growing from axils of the previous year's growth. The size of the flowers varies from a few millimetres up to 2.5cm (1in) or more in diameter. Most have short tubes, but there are a few with spectacular long-tubed flowers and these are particularly popular with growers. Following pollination, the developing fruits are retained within the body of the plant, usually not appearing until the following season. In a few rare cases, the fruits are largely retained within the body indefinitely, so making seed collection difficult.

Most mammillaria species are found in Mexico and the south-west of the USA with just a few occurring in other countries around the Caribbean. Some are widespread and exhibit considerable variation in appearance depending on where they are from. Others are very localized and are only known to grow at one small place. The diversity of habitat preferences probably accounts for the differing cultural requirements of these plants. Most species are easy to grow, but a few are amongst the most difficult of all cacti in cultivation, and of course it is these that are the most prized by collectors.

There are a number of useful reference books that describe and illustrate the species but the most recent and best illustrated is *Mammillaria* by John Pilbeam.

The small species of the mammillaria series lasiacanthae *make a pleasing collection.*

Mammillaria spinosissima *is a very easily grown, free-flowering species.*

LEFT: Mammillaria zeilmanniana *is the top-selling cactus in the UK.*

MAMMILLARIA ZEILMANNIANA

More plants of this species are grown commercially than any other cactus, principally because it has the unusual characteristic of repeatedly flowering throughout the summer. It grows quickly and easily, rapidly forming large clusters of stems that produce ring after ring of bright pink flowers. Very easy to cultivate in standard conditions and one of the best for flowers, this species was only recently rediscovered in the wild in the Mexican state of Guanajuato. A white-flowered cultivar is also extensively propagated from seed and fortunately breeds true.

Similar species: *M. mercadensis, M. bocasana*

MAMMILLARIA SPINOSISSIMA

Another classic mammillaria that produces rings of flowers in spring from large heads that cluster from the base. The straight spines of this variable species can be coloured from red to yellow and brown. It is very easy to cultivate from seed and soon makes a sizeable clump of elongated stems, which are an impressive sight with their rings of blooms. Ideal for beginners, success with this will encourage growers to try some of the more difficult species. It comes from the mountains near to Mexico City.

Similar species: *M. backebergiana, M. meyranii*

MAMMILLARIA BOMBYCINA

A few mammillarias readily grow into large clusters of stems and make impressive specimens, and this is one of the best. It is often seen at shows in a washing-up bowl or even a cut-down dustbin – which deserves a prize if only for the sheer effort of transporting it! It is a most attractive species with many white radial spines and red centrals that provide a backdrop for the freely produced, bright pink flowers. It grows rapidly from seed and if regularly potted-on will soon make a spectacular specimen. It was only recently rediscovered in the wild in the state of Aguascalientes in Mexico.

Similar species: *M. bombycina* ssp. *perezdelarosae, M. berkiana*

Mammillaria bombycina *grows into very large clusters of heads.*

MAMMILLARIA MYSTAX

Here is a species that remains solitary and can grow to 10cm (4in) or more in diameter with the symmetry that has made mammillarias so popular. It has prominent bristles in the axils between the tubercles, a feature found in many species of the genus. Easy to grow from seed and often offered for sale, this plant will produce the rings of red flowers traditionally associated with this large genus. It has an extensive habitat range in southern Mexico where various populations have been given their own names as so often happens with widespread plants.
Similar species: *M. sartorii, M. varieaculeata*

Mammillaria mystax grows its flowers in a ring around the crown typical of the genus.

Mammillaria blossfeldiana has large flowers with a prominent mid-stripe.

MAMMILLARIA BLOSSFELDIANA

This is one of the many hooked-spined mammillarias from the Baja peninsula to the west of Mexico, most of which are tricky to grow because they tend to have poor root systems in cultivation and are prone to rot. However, they are worth the effort because most species have glorious flowers, amongst the best in the genus. *M. blossfeldiana* is one of the smaller examples, usually remaining solitary in its habitat in central-west Baja, but clustering to make a group of stems up to 15cm (6in) in diameter when grown in a pot. The characteristic striped flowers are both attractive and unusual. Less than average water and a bright position in the greenhouse will give the best chance of success with this difficult species.
Similar species: *M. insularis, M. boolii*

MAMMILLARIA ALBICANS SSP. FRAILEANA

Coming from the southern tip of the Baja peninsula, this hooked spined species has large white flowers and the prominent, long stigma lobes often found in this group. It grows cylindrical stems up to 15cm (6in) in height that will form impressive but untidy clusters in time, given careful watering and a sunny location. The long stems have a tendency to become prostrate, particularly when dry. It is usually raised from seed but stems can also be used as cuttings for propagation.
Similar species: *M. hutchisoniana, M. mazatlanensis*

MAMMILLARIA THERESAE

When this plant was discovered in the late 1960s and came into cultivation, it caused quite a stir because of its long-tubed flowers and the spination, which needs to viewed under a lens to be appreciated. Plants were initially grafted, but they grew tall and lost the character of this miniature whose stems should only be up to 5cm (2in) tall. It is now raised from seed and the resulting plants flower when still tiny, the

RIGHT: Mammillaria albicans ssp. fraileana is typical of a series of mammillarias from Baja, California.

flowers of 4cm (1.5in) in length often obscuring the plant. The small seed pods are retained within the body so it is necessary to carefully dig them out to collect the few seeds they contain. It comes from Durango, Mexico.

Similar species: *M. saboae, M. saboae* ssp. *goldii, M. deherdtiana*

MAMMILLARIA CRUCIGERA

Here is a plant for the patient grower since it can take more than ten years to make a good cluster of stems. However, it is not difficult to grow and the small flowers will appear when the plant is still quite young; then in later life the flowers will form a ring half-way down the stem from areoles that grow extra wool. It forms clumps by multiplying dichotomously when the growing point divides into two, a phenomenon seen in many mammillarias and occasionally in other genera. Much prized on the show bench because of its slow growth, this plant naturally grows on gypsum cliffs in Puebla and Oaxaca, Mexico.

MAMMILLARIA CARMENAE

This beautifully spined plant was discovered in the middle of the twentieth century but was soon lost to cultivation; some twenty-five years later it was re-discovered in Tamaulipas, Mexico, and introduced into our collections by means of seedlings that proved to be easy to grow. It is a shame that there is so little contrast between

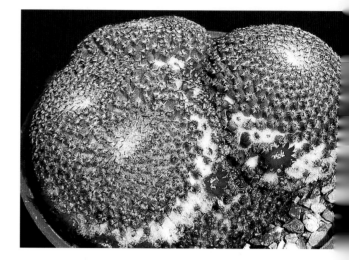

Mammillaria crucigera *grows new heads by division at the growing point.*

the freely produced rings of white flowers and the spines, but you can solve this by growing one of the pink-flowered hybrids with *M. laui*, which is described below (see page 34). Also in cultivation now are forms with reddish spines that are said to originate from the wild.

MAMMILLARIA LAUI

Closely related to *M. carmenae* and growing not far away from it in Tamaulipas, Mexico, this species was found while Alfred Lau was looking for *M. carmenae* and subsequently named for him. It comes in three forms separated by altitude; the higher you climb, the softer the spines

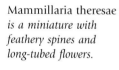

Mammillaria theresae *is a miniature with feathery spines and long-tubed flowers.*

LEFT: Mammillaria carmenae *has only recently been re-discovered in Mexico.*

BELOW: Mammillaria laui, *a beautiful clump-forming species that is easy to cultivate.*

BOTTOM: Mammillaria formosa *ssp.* chionocephala *has heads with bands of white woolly areoles.*

and the more caespitose the plants become. They are all straightforward to grow in a sunny spot and flower freely in the early months of the year, the high-altitude form such as the one illustrated being particularly easy to grow into big clusters of small stems.

MAMMILLARIA FORMOSA SSP. CHIONOCEPHALA

This is a solitary species most notable for the large amount of white wool in the axils between the tubercles. It grows well from seed to make a stem some 15cm (6in) in height with bands of wool around it corresponding to where the rings of flowers were produced. It presents no difficulty when raised from seed and the pretty white flowers are first produced on seedlings about 8cm (3in) in diameter. Its extensive natural habitat is in north-east Mexico.

MAMMILLARIA HUMBOLDTII

Surely one of the most beautiful of all cacti, this slow-growing species has the most wonderful white spines and contrasting deep pink flowers. There are at least two different forms in cultivation, one making clusters of small heads and another where the heads grow larger and cluster less freely, as in the illustration. In cultivation it needs a sunny place and less water than

109

Mammillaria humboldtii *is one of the best white-spined species.*

smaller in its native home in the Mexican state of San Luis Potosi. There is more of the plant below ground than above and the tuberous root is prone to rot if damaged, so great care must be taken when re-potting. Careful watering in the summer and a sunny location will reward the grower with quite large white flowers produced in early spring. The soft, hair-like spines can be white or pale yellow depending on the clone.

Similar species: *M. lenta*

MAMMILLARIA PECTINIFERA

Plants with pectinate spines are always popular and this would be among the top ten favourite cacti of many enthusiasts. It is easy to confuse with *Turbinicarpus pseudopectinatus* until the pale

average to avoid problems with rot. A good layer of grit under the bodies helps to keep them dry and avoids staining of the lower parts of the plant by water, which can be drawn up among the spines. It comes from the Mexican state of Hidalgo where it grows on limestone.

Mammillaria aureilanata *has a large underground stem and soft radial spines.*

MAMMILLARIA AUREILANATA

Another slow-growing species, this plant remains solitary and grows to about 8cm (3in) across in cultivation, although it is said to remain much

Mammillaria pectinifera *would be among the top ten favourite plants of many collectors.*

yellow flowers appear in a ring, confirming its status as a mammillaria. With patience it can be raised from seed and although slow to grow, the seedlings will produce the odd flower when only a couple of centimetres across. It remains solitary and given sunshine and careful watering it will eventually reach 5cm (2in) in diameter, a significant achievement for any grower as it becomes more difficult to cultivate when it gets to half that size. It is difficult to see in its homeland in Puebla, Mexico as it grows flush with the ground in limestone.

Mammillaria guelzowiana *has the most spectacular flowers in the genus.*

MAMMILLARIA GUELZOWIANA

This mammillaria has just about the largest flowers of all but it is tricky to cultivate and prone to rot. It needs to be watered with care, only in warm weather and only when the soil is dry from the last watering. However, given favourable conditions, it will grow quickly from seed and make a cluster of heads covered with soft white hair through which protrude the red or yellow hooked spines. It is a splendid sight when covered with its bright magenta-pink flowers, one of the highlights of the growing year. Its natural home is in the Mexican state of Durango.

MAMMILLARIA SENILIS

This is a most individual species, its large and unusually shaped flowers distinguishing it from all other mammillarias, a characteristic that prompted the erection of the genus mamillopsis to accommodate it alone. Given a sunny place it is not difficult to grow, and will make a large clump of heads given time. The bright red flowers, which appear very early in the year, are not freely produced in all collections and it is thought that good winter light might be the key to superior flowering. There is a white-flowered sport in cultivation but it is only a curiosity, certainly not as impressive as the usual form. In habitat it can be found at high altitude throughout a large area of central-north Mexico.

MAMMILLARIA PONDII

There are a few species of mammillaria that have evolved to be pollinated by humming-birds and these were once in their own genus – cochemiea. All from Baja, Mexico, they need the sunniest place you can find, then they will grow into large clusters of heavily spined, elongated stems. The flowers are very bright red and tubular with shining reflexed petals but they are not produced reliably unless you have a good clone, then you can look forward to flowers all through the summer. Easily raised from seed, they usually need to be a good size before they will bloom for the first time.

Similar species: *M. halei, M. poselgeri*

Mammillaria senilis, *as well as having white spines, has unusual large red flowers.*

Mammillaria pondii *is one of the few mammillarias pollinated by humming-birds.*

MAMMILLARIA SCHUMANNII

The final example of the genus described here is one of the best. Like *M. albicans* ssp. *fraileana* it comes from the southern tip of the Baja peninsular and has the same spectacular flowers. Its outstanding features are its ability to form neat clusters of short stems and, in the best forms, its pale blue-green body covered with white spines, which is attractive even out of flower. Tricky to grow, but a sunny location, careful watering and at least 10°C (50°F) in winter will aid successful cultivation. It is usually raised from seed and the seedlings will flower when small, just 3cm (1in) or so in diameter.

Matucana

Now very popular, these plants were almost unobtainable before the 1970s when exploration of South America made them available to collectors. They all come from Peru, some inhabiting the highlands and others the warm inland valleys, the latter tending to have fewer spines.

They nearly all have beautiful long-tubed flowers that have evolved for pollination by humming-birds, only a few having regular flowers for bees. Humming-bird flowers are more usually associated with large-growing columnar cacti, so to be able to enjoy these unusual flowers on small globular plants is a great attraction for collectors. Some species will flower repeatedly through the summer whilst others bloom most in the late summer when there are few other cacti in bloom.

Easy to grow, the only special consideration is extra winter warmth for some of the lowland species such as the unique *M. madisoniorum*. The usual propagation method is by raising seed although some species clump freely, the offsets often growing roots whilst still attached to the main stem. The interesting genus oroya is included here because it requires similar conditions in cultivation.

Mammillaria baumii has large yellow flowers that are unusual in the genus.

MAMMILLARIA BAUMII

Large yellow flowers are not found on many mammillaria species and this one, among others, was formerly included in the genus dolichothele. This pretty species is one of the best with its white spines and scented flowers, easily making a large cluster of heads. It can be raised from seed or grown from cuttings and presents no problems in cultivation if given a bright situation. For some reason it is not as popular now as it used to be, but it is a good choice for collectors new to the hobby. It comes from Tamaulipas, Mexico where it grows in woodland.

Mammillaria schumannii is tricky to grow well but rewards the effort.

MATUCANA HAYNEI

This widespread plant grows at high altitude in the coastal mountains of Peru. The bodies are covered with dense, usually white, spines. Some

Matucana haynei comes from the high Andes and has humming-bird pollinated flowers.

Matucana paucicostata *makes large clumps of stems and flowers easily.*

forms grow long stems that will eventually become prostrate while others make large clusters of globose heads. It is easy to grow in a sunny place but some clones can be reluctant to flower.

Similar species: *M. weberbaueri, M. comacephala*

MATUCANA PAUCICOSTATA

Probably the commonest in cultivation because it is easy to grow and quick to propagate from offsets, this is one of the sparsely spined species from the inland valleys of Peru. It prefers a minimum temperature of 10°C (50°F) in winter and should be given adequate moisture in summer when its unusual flowers are freely produced.

Similar species: *M. aurantiaca, M. krahnii, M. pujupatii*

OROYA PERUVIANA

The genus oroya is found at high altitude in Peru, growing in open grassland and among rocks. It is a very cold place in winter and receives plenty

of water in the summer so these plants are not difficult to cultivate. They need to be kept moist in summer and a little water in winter will help to stop them becoming dehydrated, which can adversely affect the flowering in early spring. The stems rarely offset and can grow to 15cm (6in) in diameter but will sometimes flower when only half that size. The small flowers, which are often bi-coloured, can be produced in large numbers around the crown.

Similar species: *O. borchersii*

Oroya peruviana *from the high Andes often has bi-coloured flowers.*

Melocactus

This remarkable genus is unique in growing a terminal cephalium from which small red flowers emerge during the day. The cephalium is a distinctly different form of growth produced at maturity purely for the production of flowers and subsequently fruit. When young, Melocacti are globular and ribbed with areoles much like other cacti, then after some years, the normal body stops growing and the cephalium appears from the growing point. After that only the cephalium grows and in some species it can reach a considerable height, flowering regularly in a ring near the top. Most species are self fertile and the fruits are squeezed out of the cephalium, often in large numbers. These are red in most species, but a few are white. Most species come from Brazil but others occur across a wide distribution through the Caribbean and down the west side of South America as far as Peru. They grow in hot places so require a winter minimum of 10°C (50°F), some even more. They are not difficult to grow so long as they are kept warm enough and not over-potted. They seem to enjoy having their roots constricted so that the compost dries out quickly and this can be achieved by using shallow pots. Potting on should be done carefully and the new pot should not be too large, particularly if the plant already has a cephalium. There are very many species of Melocactus, a genus which is not a good choice for the beginner, but an experienced collector can find a challenge with these extraordinary plants.

Melocactus azureus, *a mature plant such as this is rare in cultivation.*

A useful review by Nigel Taylor can be found in *Bradleya* 9, 1991 and is available as an extracted reprint.

MELOCACTUS MATANZANUS

One of the smallest of the genus, this neat species comes from Cuba. It is extensively cultivated for the horticultural trade because it grows its cephalium when only about five years old and about 10cm (4in) in diameter. It has tiny flowers which appear in a ring around the centre of the cephalium and are followed by red fruits. It is among the easier species to grow and so long as a minimum of 15°C (60°F) is maintained, it will grow without difficulty. The seeds germinate easily and the young seedlings should be left to grow to a reasonable size before being pricked out.

MELOCACTUS AZUREUS

This species like many others comes from eastern Brazil and it is among the most beautiful and one of the largest. It has a reputation for being difficult to cultivate and so is often grafted, a good way to grow it successfully. The blue colour of the epidermis is unusual in the genus and is highly prized by collectors. It is one of

Melocactus matanzanus, *one of the smallest species, in cultivation in the Netherlands.*

the species with white fruits and in its habitat it grows on limestone outcrops. Seed grows readily but it takes many years before the plant grows to over 20cm (8in) tall so becoming large enough to mature and produce a cephalium.

Similar species: *M. pachyacanthus*

Mexican Treasures

Probably the most desirable of all cacti, these slow-growing species have always been prized by collectors. The demand had been satisfied for decades by the importation of mature plants from the wild, but this resulted in many becoming threatened with extinction. Most are now included in Appendix 1 of CITES, the most threatened category, and protected from commercial exploitation. However, their desirability means that there is still an illegal traffic in smuggled plants that continues to threaten the survival of the rarer Mexican species. It is encouraging to hear that new populations of some species have been found and it can only be hoped that these locations can be kept secret from those who would steal the plants.

This informal grouping of choice species includes ariocarpus, turbinicarpus and a number of small genera that are all very popular with collectors, probably because of their slow growth and interesting form. These same characteristics make them successful at shows where wonderful specimens of great age can often be seen and admired (see page 31).

It is one of the great challenges in the hobby to grow all the ariocarpus species from seed to flowering size, which in the UK can take anything up to eight years. The genus contains true miniature species such as *A. kotschoubeyanus* as well as a few that can grow quite large, even making clusters, for example *A. retusus*. This latter species has a very extensive distribution in habitat whereas some others are very localized, which has made their survival vulnerable to illegal collecting. This situation has resulted in all ariocarpus species being listed in Appendix 1 of CITES. Since this ruling and the ban by Mexico on the export of seed, a new species, *A. bravoanus*, has been described from a single, small population, but because of the regulations it is practically impossible to obtain this plant legally outside Mexico. Regrettably, the desire of some collectors to have rare plants, irrespective of the consequences, has led to the illegal removal of most of the plants from the habitat, which might mean that this unique species will become extinct in the wild.

Cultivation is not difficult but requires great patience and a sunny location in a glasshouse. Peat-based soils are not suitable for the long-term maintenance of these species, which should be grown in Mexican mix (see page 45). Seed is the usual method of propagation even though the seedlings can be very slow growing when young. Although some of the various turbinicarpus will flower when only two years old, it could take ten years to raise an aztekium to flowering size and the plant will still be less than 2cm (0.75in) in diameter. All the pictures in this section are of plants grown from seed in the UK under ordinary glasshouse conditions.

A good read on this subject is *The Threatened Cacti of Mexico* by Anderson et al. Also, the recently published *Ariocarpus etc.* by John Pilbeam describes all these and some other desirable species.

ARIOCARPUS FISSURATUS

One of the smaller species of ariocarpus, this is the only one that grows in the USA as well as Mexico, where all the other species can be found. The form found in the northern part of its range makes solitary heads that grow flush with the ground up to 6cm (2.5in) in diameter, but a form from the south, originally called *A. lloydii*, can get much larger. It can take six years to reach flowering size at about 4cm (1.5in) in diameter when grown in a sunny place with less than average water. Like all species of the genus, it grows most and flowers in the autumn.

Ariocarpus fissuratus, *grown from seed and flowering in a 7cm (2.75in) pot.*

ARIOCARPUS AGAVOIDES

Another small-growing solitary species, this is easily raised from seed and will first flower when only about four years old with just a few of its characteristic long tubercles. This plant is extensively grown in cultivation and sometimes grafted, a practice that rarely produces a natural looking specimen of any ariocarpus and so is not recommended. It is difficult to see in its natural habitat in eastern Mexico except when flowering.

Ariocarpus agavoides, grown from seed and flowering in a 7cm (2.75in) pot.

BELOW Ariocarpus trigonus, grown from seed and flowering in an 8cm (3in) pot.

ARIOCARPUS TRIGONUS

The characteristics of this desirable plant are its long tubercles and yellow flowers that are not found in any other species in the genus. The individual heads can grow to 30cm (12in) in diameter making this one of the largest species, but it is slow growing in cultivation and one of the last to flower when grown from seed. Originating in the Mexican state of Tamaulipas, this species is rarely found in cultivation, perhaps because the plants that used to be imported from the wild proved difficult to establish.

ARIOCARPUS RETUSUS

This is the easiest and quickest ariocarpus to grow and the one that can make the largest plants because of its clumping habit. Over its extensive habitat range in eastern Mexico it is a variable plant both in its tubercle shape and also its flower colour, which is usually white but can also be red. Some forms with long tubercles look like *A. trigonus* and these can have magenta red flowers. Raised from seed, this species will flower when 6cm (2.5in) in diameter at about six years of age.

ABOVE Ariocarpus retusus, grown from seed and flowering in a 10cm (4in) pot.

Strombocactus disciformis, *grown from seed and flowering in a 6cm (2.5in) pot.*

STROMBOCACTUS DISCIFORMIS

A most individual plant from Hidalgo, Mexico, where it grows on steep limestone cliffs. It is very slow growing – a forty-year-old plant would probably fit in a 9cm (3.5in) pot. The seeds are extremely tiny, so the young seedlings are very small and grow slowly for the first few years of life. Once they are a centimetre or so across they start to grow more quickly and a flowering plant can be obtained in about eight years after which, if well grown, it will start to look like the adult plants that used to be imported. The flowers are white but the recent discovery of red-flowered plants has been greeted with much excitement.

PELECYPHORA STROBILIFORMIS

Another 'classic' cactus, this very slow-growing species has been coveted by collectors for decades. Its cultivation is not difficult but you need extreme patience if you are to raise it from seed since it will take more than ten years to grow to 3cm (1in) in diameter. It can be grown from offsets, which are occasionally produced on mature plants, and this is quicker than seed but still a slow process. Highly regarded at shows because of its great age, care needs to be taken to avoid the ends of the tubercles drying up if the plant is to win a prize. It is also prone to red spider attack, from which it can take years to recover (see page 52).

OBREGONIA DENEGRII

This is the only species in the genus obregonia – a very individual plant and one that takes well to cultivation. Although it looks quite like an ariocarpus, it is quicker to raise from seed and flowers when about five years old, then regularly throughout the summer. It does not make offsets and the body can eventually grow to 10cm (4in) in diameter. The centres of well-grown specimens become very woolly, much more so than in the wild. It comes from Tamaulipas, Mexico.

Pelecyphora strobiliformis *flowering in a 5cm (2in) pot.*

Obregonia denegrii *grows masses of white wool in the crown when cultivated under glass.*

EPITHELANTHA MICROMERIS

A number of forms of this densely spined small cactus grow in the southern USA and northern Mexico. Some remain solitary, others can make large clusters of stems but these take many years in cultivation to grow. This beautiful and unusual species must be grown from seed. Flowering can be achieved in just a few years, but the blooms are small and less spectacular than the long red fruits that are freely produced. A warm and sunny location with less than average watering will produce the best results.

LOPHOPHORA WILLIAMSII

The areoles of this plant have tufts of wool in place of spines and the pink or white flowers appear from the young areoles in the crown. When grown from seed it can be expected to flower when about 3cm (1in) in diameter and then sporadically throughout the summer. It needs full sun and care in watering at the beginning of the growing season since it is prone to split if over-watered. Red spider mite can cause serious damage to the blue-green epidermis causing it to scar. It is native to Mexico where it can grow into large clusters but can also be found in the extreme south of the USA.

TURBINICARPUS SCHMIEDICKEANUS

One of a number of small, easily grown plants from Mexico that are very popular with collectors because of their willingness to flower when young. All its forms can be grown from seed without difficulty and will sometimes flower when only two years old. The flowers are white, pink or yellow and an interesting collection can be accumulated in a small area of greenhouse staging. Some will make small clusters of stems whilst others grow larger solitary bodies. A bright place is required for the best results.

Similar species: *T. pseudomacrochele, T. swobodae*

ABOVE Turbinicarpus schmiedickeanus *is a free-flowering miniature species.*

Turbinicarpus pseudopectinatus *has neat pectinate spines and pretty flowers.*

TURBINICARPUS PSEUDOPECTINATUS

Another example of a small-growing turbinicarpus but this has particularly attractive pectinate spines, reminiscent of *Mammillaria pectinifera* except that the flowers are borne on areoles in the centre of the plant like all species in this genus. When raised from seed, the plant can produce white or sometimes pinkish blooms when still very small.

Similar species: *T. valdezianus*

TURBINICARPUS BEGUINII

A number of species of turbinicarpus were once in a genus called gymnocactus of which this is an example. These plants are generally larger growing than other species of turbinicarpus and this one makes solitary heads up to 15cm (6in) in height. Its pink flowers contrast well with the white spines. It comes from Coahuila, Mexico.

Similar species: *T. gielsdorfianus, T. zaragozae*

Turbinicarpus beguinii *is covered with glassy white spines.*

119

Opuntia

This is the largest genus of cacti, with over 400 accepted species that occur naturally across the distribution range of the family as a whole. When opuntia is mentioned, most people think of the prickly pear (platyopuntia) with its characteristic fleshy stems made up of flat pads. These have been introduced to most parts of the world where the climate is suitable and have become a familiar sight in Australia, Africa and around the Mediterranean. As well as the edible fruit, they have many practical uses including cattle feed, field boundaries and as a host to the cochineal beetle used for making red food dye. However, the pads easily break off and take root on the ground resulting in the rapid colonization of vast areas of land, so making the prickly pear a serious pest. The management of this problem in Australia by the introduction of natural predators is one of the classic examples of biological control.

Such fast-growing species can rapidly outgrow their welcome. It usually comes as a surprise to the novice that any cactus can grow that fast, particularly if it is planted directly into the ground rather than a pot. However, one should not dismiss opuntias as unsuitable for glasshouse culture since there are many attractive small-growing types that

add diversity to the ranks of the globular and columnar cacti. Most of these desirable species do not have flat pads but cylindrical stems or globular to ovate stem sections. The flowers are all particularly beautiful with a wide range of colours and the challenge of getting them to bloom under glass is one of the attractions. They need the sunniest location possible with cool, bright winters to encourage flowering and to stop the stem segments elongating unnaturally, which is always a risk under glass. Many are frost hardy if kept reasonably dry so an unheated greenhouse or a cold frame can be suitable. One unattractive feature, which is only found in opuntia, is the presence of glochids. These tiny, easily detached spines are equipped with barbs so that they penetrate your skin but are difficult to remove. Extreme care must be taken when working with these plants or you can suffer discomfort for days.

Opuntia has been divided into a number of sub-genera, the names of which are frequently used by amateur growers. Those most often seen are cylindropuntia, grusonia, maihueniopsis, pterocactus and tephrocactus, and for convenience these are used below. The following species include examples of all the main types that are suitable for glasshouse culture. Most are propagated as cuttings rather than seedlings since the

Opuntias are famous for their spiny, flat stem sections known as 'pads'.

seed is rarely available of the choice small-growing plants and it can be difficult to germinate.

There has not been a comprehensive book published about opuntia so it is necessary to look in various cactus society journals and general publications to find more information. The genus is currently very popular and has its own specialist study group.

Opuntia

This includes the flat-padded plants that are the most familiar stem form of this extensive genus. They are not the best choice for cultivation but the interesting shape has made *O. microdasys* one of the best selling of all cacti. It looks innocent enough since it lacks long spines, but in fact the areoles are very well furnished with glochids that rub off easily and cause irritaion of the skin for days. It only flowers if given a very sunny position, so it is more likely to give cacti a bad name than create a convert to the hobby. A few species, such as *O. azurea*, are hardy enough to be permanently planted outdoors in the milder parts of the UK so long as they are prevented from becoming too wet in winter. This can be achieved by positioning them near a south-facing wall in well-drained soil where they will receive any available sun. All opuntias of this type are easy to root by removing pads as cuttings, which, if taken from a mature plant, will often continue to flower.

Opuntia microdasys *might look harmless but each areole is full of tiny barbed spines.*

Opuntia azurea *is hardy and can be grown outside if protected from excess water.*

Opuntia basilaris *growing in habitat in Nevada shows the beauty of opuntia flowers.*

Grusonia

Once only applied to a few species, this name has now been expanded to include species previously in the genera corynopuntia and micropuntia. They come from Mexico and the USA and often have spectacular spination. They make good pot plants for a sunny location and many will flower at a manageable size. Particularly popular is *G. invicta*, a native of Baja, which has large ovoid joints from which the bright red young spines emerge. A slow-growing plant that can take many years to make a good cluster of stems, it is propagated from cuttings but it can take a long time to root a severed joint.

Other suggested species: *G. clavata, G. bulbispina*

BELOW: Grusonia invicta *has dense spines that are bright red when they first emerge.*

BOTTOM: Grusonia bulbispina *is a small species that will flower if given enough sun.*

Tephrocactus

Probably the most popular of all small opuntias, these South American plants are easy to grow in a bright place and some can be expected to flower in a glasshouse. They are propagated by removing joints that will root without difficulty. In fact, *T. articulatus* will often shed its joints in the wild, which then root on the ground to make new plants. This species usually has soft papery spines although some forms can be spineless. The choice *T. alexanderi* ssp. *geometricus* has very neatly spined joints and lovely pink flowers. It will only grow one or two new segments each year, so it takes some time to grow to a good size.

Other suggested species: *T. molinensis, T. weberi*

Tephrocactus articulatus *from Argentina has flexible, papery spines.*

Tephrocactus alexanderi *ssp.* geometricus *is easy to grow but difficult to find for sale.*

Maihueniopsis

Another genus from South America, these are high-altitude plants capable of withstanding cold winters so long as they are kept dry. Used to strong sunshine in their natural home, they must be given the brightest available place in cultivation to prevent the stems elongating and to promote flowering. Like many alpine plants, some species such as *M. glomerata*, make tightly packed low hummocks as an adaptation to the extreme climate but they do it to a lesser degree in cultivation. The small-growing species *M. subterranea* has long, swollen roots with only a small part of the plant above ground. It flowers freely in a range of pastel pink shades and makes an ideal pot plant.

Other suggested species: *M. clavarioides, M. mandragora*

Pterocactus

Coming from the southern part of Argentina, this is the most individual of all these genera. It has large tuberous roots from which cylindrical stems grow and eventually bloom at their

tips. The flowers, which are unusual shades of yellow or pink, appear to be a continuation of the stems. These are followed by fruits packed with winged seeds ('ptero' means winged). They are easy to grow and tolerant of cold, but the root tubers are best raised above the ground in cultivation to reduce the risk of rotting. Cuttings of the stems root easily and produce their own tubers in time.

TOP: Maihueniopsis glomerata *makes large mounds of stems and needs a sunny location.*

ABOVE: Maihueniopsis subterranea *is an easy miniature species to grow.*

123

Pterocactus tuberosus *has a large swollen root and flowers of unusual colours.*

Pterocactus australis *comes from Patagonia and will survive low temperatures if kept dry.*

Parodia

This large genus originates from a large area of central South America and includes many beautiful plants. Many species that were long known as notocactus, eriocactus and brasilicactus are now included here since they have all recently been incorporated into the older genus parodia. Another genus, frailea, is also mentioned here because the plants are similar to some parodias, the main difference being their small size.

All species are easy to grow and flower so they make excellent beginners' plants. Most should be shaded from strong sunlight for at least part of the day and given plenty of water in the growing season. The standard soil mix (see page 45) is ideal and regular feeding will produce the best results with these hungry plants that are sensitive to alkalinity of the growing medium. Seed raising is straightforward if the young plants are kept moist for the first few months, although the small-seeded species like *P. microsperma* are very tiny indeed when young and take some time to really start growing well.

The only English-language book about notocactus is now rather out of date. The most recent and complete treatment is *Notokakteen* by Gerloff et al. The three-volumes by Weskamp is only suitable for the very keen. A small band of notocactus enthusiasts in continental Europe run a specialist group.

PARODIA MICROSPERMA

Found naturally in Argentina, the various populations of this widespread plant have been given very many names. It is a small, solitary plant in nature, rarely exceeding 4cm (1.5in) in diameter, but in cultivation it can get much larger. It enjoys constant moisture in the growing season when it will accept some shade from the full intensity of the sun. Flowers are produced in profusion from the centre of the plant throughout the summer and can be yellow or red. The neat hooked spines and bright flowers make this a popular choice for the collector.

Similar species: *P. microsperma* ssp. *horrida*

Parodia microsperma *(sanguiniflora) flowers profusely in spring.*

Parodia microsperma *has tiny seeds that take some time to grow to any size.*

PARODIA CHRYSACANTHION

Another native of Argentina, this is found in a small region in the north of the country. Before the amalgamation of notocactus, it was one of the few straight-spined species of parodia. Frequently seen in collections, it grows solitary heads densely covered in golden spines up to 15cm (6in) across in cultivation but remains much smaller in habitat where it grows on steep, rocky hillsides, sometimes under trees. It is sold in large numbers commercially so should not be difficult to buy as a flowering size plant.
Similar species: *P. nivosa, P. penicillata*

PARODIA TUBERCULATA

One example of the many parodias from Bolivia, this one is easy to flower at a small size. The red flowers, produced from young areoles in the crown, are a good contrast with the white woolly areoles. These species with larger seeds grow more quickly than others in the genus and will flower when only three years old. A sunny location and adequate water in summer will produce a free-flowering specimen that remains solitary and grows to 7cm (2.75in) in diameter.
Similar species: *P. taratensis, P. schwebsiana*

Parodia chrysacanthion *is a favourite species among growers.*

Parodia tuberculata *grows easily and flowers when still a small plant.*

Parodia herteri can become very large and has lovely pink flowers.

PARODIA HERTERI

This plant is best known as a large-growing species of the genus notocactus. It comes from the border region of Brazil and Uruguay where it can grow to 20cm (8in) in diameter and is unusual for having pink blooms whilst most of its close relatives are yellow flowered. Seed raising is the only way to propagate this solitary species, but the seedlings need to be at least 10cm (4in) in diameter before they will flower. A generous supply of water and fertilizer in summer will soon make an impressive specimen.

Similar species: *P. horstii*

PARODIA OTTONIS

A very well known and popular plant most often seen under its old name *Notocactus ottonis*, this species is very widespread in Uruguay and southern Brazil. It grows quickly from seed to form large clusters of globular heads, which can easily be detached for propagation, often already having their own root system. The large yellow flowers have a wonderful sheen in the sun and are produced throughout the summer. It enjoys plenty of water in the summer and some shade from strong sunlight. There are many names for the various forms of this species including the red-flowered *P. ottonis venclusianus*.

Similar species: *P. linkii, P. tenuicylindrica, P. oxycostata*

Parodia ottonis is widespread in Uruguay and southern Brazil where it makes big clusters.

PARODIA WERNERI

Since most species of the genus notocactus known at the time had yellow flowers, the discovery of this species in 1966 caused much interest because of its beautiful purple flowers. It was then named *N. uebelmannianus* and it was reported that some plants in the population had yellow flowers, both forms still being in cultivation. It is straightforward to grow from seed and easily flowers when only 5cm (2in) in diameter, always remaining solitary and eventually growing to 12cm (5in).

Similar species: *P. crassigibba*

RIGHT: Parodia werneri can have purple or yellow flowers.

PARODIA SCOPA

This variable species was discovered long ago growing near Montivideo in Uruguay, later being included in the genus notocactus. It has a dense covering of spines, most of them white but with dark centrals. The bodies can grow to be very tall, eventually falling over and becoming prostrate. Offsets are sometimes formed following the abortion of flower buds so that a clump of stems results. The pretty yellow flowers make a ring around the crown of old specimens and help to make this a favourite of many growers. It presents no problems in cultivation but can suffer from stem constrictions if kept too dry.

Similar species: *P. rudibuenekeri*, *P. scopa* ssp. *succinea*

Parodia scopa is covered with dense white spines and can grow into a large specimen.

PARODIA HASELBERGII

One of the best cacti of all for the beginner, this white-spined plant is spectacular when blooming, the bright red of the flowers contrasting beautifully with the glassy spines. As a bonus, the flowers are among the longest lasting of any cactus, over a week in favourable conditions. The plant was once in the genus brasilicactus and comes from southern Brazil where it grows on steep, moist rock faces. Cultivated plants get much larger than those in the wild, becoming splendid specimens of up to 15cm (6in) in diameter.

Similar species: *P. haselbergii* ssp. *graessneri*

PARODIA MAGNIFICA

An example of a distinct group of species once in the genus eriocactus, this architectural plant is commonly seen in collections. It can be found in southern Brazil where it lives in dense stands on steep rocks. It is very easy to cultivate and given adequate root space and plenty of water in summer it will grow very quickly and flower repeatedly. The bluish body and continuous woolly edge to the ribs makes this a very distinctive species that will eventually offset to make a large clump. It is slightly sensitive to cold and a minimum temperature of 10°C (50°F) is recommended in winter.

Similar species: *P. warasii*, *P. schumanniana*

Parodia haselbergii has flowers that can last longer than any other cactus.

Parodia magnifica quickly grows into large clusters that flower all summer.

PARODIA LENINGHAUSII

Closely related to *P. magnifica* but much taller and with more ribs, this popular species has been in cultivation for many years – most collections have at least one specimen and it is often seen at shows. It needs plenty of root space and frequent watering in the summer, when it will grow quickly to form clusters of columnar heads, each with a sloping crown. In habitat it grows on nearly inaccessible steep rock slopes in southern Brazil.

Parodia leninghausii is a beautiful species and one of the most popular of all cacti.

Frailea pygmaea, *one of the smallest cacti, which can also be short-lived.*

FRAILEA PYGMAEA

The genus frailea comprises a number of species from Brazil, Uruguay and Paraguay that are among the smallest of all cacti. They grow in moist places where the soil is shallow, such as at the edge of rock plates in regions where deeper soil allows grasses, shrubs and even trees to grow. Flowering-sized plants can be just a centimetre across but such small specimens, or those that are dehydrated, rarely open their flowers. They have evolved the moisture-saving ability to set seed even when the flowers remain closed, a process called cleistogamy. This is rarely found elsewhere in the family *Cactaceae*. A shady place and adequate water will give the best chance of producing the yellow flowers.

Similar species: *F. pumila, F. cataphracta, F. castanea*

Rebutia

Another large genus from South America that includes some of the easiest cacti to cultivate. Always recommended for beginners, these plants usually produce offsets that can be rooted as cuttings to make more plants. The sheer quantity of brightly coloured flowers, even on young plants, provides a splash of colour in early spring and includes shades of red, pink, white, and yellow, some strong and others pastel. Particularly popular are the species better known as sulcorebutia for which there are many enthusiastic collectors. These small-growing cacti from the Bolivian Andes often have attractive spination and body colours that add to their appeal when they are not in flower. Also included here is the former genus weingartia, some species of which produce large heads and even grow into clusters with rings of yellow or occasionally red flowers.

The standard soil mix (see page 45) suits these plants well and they appreciate being kept just moist throughout the growing season with occasional feeding for best growth. They can be grown in full sun or partial shade but high temperatures should be avoided. They are susceptible to attack by red spider mite which can quickly turn the epidermis brown and scarred, a condition that takes some time to grow out and can be fatal (see page 52).

The best book about rebutia is by John Pilbeam, and for sulcorebutia and weingartia his *Collector's Guide* is the most recent English-language publication. The German-language sulcorebutia book by Augustin et al. is beautifully illustrated and excellent for the enthusiast.

REBUTIA WESSNERIANA

One of the larger growing species, this classic rebutia will eventually grow into a large cluster of white-spined heads each about 6cm (2.5in) in diameter. The large, bright red flowers are easily produced on small plants in a ring near the base. It can be grown from seed or cuttings in the usual way and, if kept well supplied with water in the summer, will soon grow into an impressive specimen. It comes from northern Argentina where it grows on steep hillsides, sometimes under sparse trees.

Similar species: *R. minuscula, R. xanthocarpa*

REBUTIA MARSONERI

Similar to *R. wessneriana* and also from northern Argentina, this is the most frequently grown yellow-flowered rebutia of the large-bodied type. It also makes big clusters of stems; each head broader than it is high. The flowers are borne in large numbers in a ring near to the base of the plant. Propagation is from seed or cuttings and the plants will take plenty of water in the growing season if given a bright, lightly shaded locality.

REBUTIA PYGMAEA

The most commonly seen example of the group of rebutias known as mediolobivia, this is a very variable and widespread species that has been given many names over the years. It has finger-sized stems that offset to make small clusters. The flowers are produced from areoles near the base of the stems. They can be red, yellow, pink or anywhere in between but white flowers are the most unusual. They are always a pastel shade and the miniature nature of this species makes it very attractive to the collector. It comes from high altitude in Bolivia and northern Argentina.

Similar species: *R. einsteinii, R. torquata*

TOP: Rebutia wessneriana *is a good plant for beginners and will flower easily.*

ABOVE: Rebutia marsoneri *is among the best yellow-flowered species.*

129

Rebutia pygmaea *can have flowers of various colours.*

REBUTIA ALBOPECTINATA

An example of a number of species once in the genus aylostera but now within rebutia. They are found in Bolivia and northern Argentina where they often grow at high altitude. This plant has smaller bodies than most but the very bright red flowers are typical of this group. It can be grown from rooted heads or from seed, and it first flowers when only a few centimetres across. Another simple plant to cultivate, its neat white spination makes it attractive even when out of flower.

Rebutia
albopectinata *from
Bolivia makes neat
clumps of small heads.*

   Similar species: *R. perplexa, R. fabrisii, R. heliosa*

REBUTIA CANIGUERALII SSP. RAUSCHII

Perhaps the most attractive of all the species originally included in the genus sulcorebutia, this plant has many beautiful body forms, all with the same shining violet flowers. The epidermis of the plant can be pale green, dark green or purple and is complimented by the black pectinate spination. A sunny location and normal watering in summer will result in a flat clump of neat bodies from which the flowers will appear in spring. Propagation is usually by cuttings to ensure that the attributes of a particular clone are passed on to the new plant. It grows at high altitude in Bolivia.

Rebutia canigueralii *ssp.* rauschii *is very popular at shows because of its body colours.*

REBUTIA CANIGUERALII

Another very variable and widespread species from Bolivia, much like *R. canigueralii* ssp. *rauschii* in habit and cultural requirements. Its main attraction is its flowers that can be red, yellow and often bi-coloured as in the illustration. Of course it is impossible to know what colour the flowers will be, so to get a particular colour, you have to get a cutting off a plant in flower.

   Similar species: *R. steinbachii*

Rebutia canigueralii *can have very spectacular flowers.*

REBUTIA ARENACEA

This Bolivian species, better known as a sulcorebutia, is quite consistent in its appearance and flower colour. The neatly spined stems are larger growing than *R. canigueralii* and form taller growing clusters. The flowers, which are always yellow, make a ring around the base of the plant in spring. It is easy to grow from cuttings or seed and is best grown in a bright place in the greenhouse.

Similar species: *R. caineana*

Rebutia arenacea *has very neat spination and yellow flowers.*

REBUTIA MENTOSA SSP. PURPUREA

Unlike most of the species formerly in the genus sulcorebutia, this plant can grow large solitary heads before offsetting sparingly. It is free-flowering, producing its pink or red blooms in a ring around the shoulder. It is usually grown from seed since offsets are only occasionally available, and will start to flower when about four years old and 5cm (2in) in diameter. It is found at high altitude in Bolivia. In cultivation, it will develop its best spination in a sunny location.

Rebutia mentosa *ssp.* purpurea *reliably produces a ring of flowers every spring.*

131

REBUTIA NEOCUMINGII

Well known under the genus name weingartia, this variable Bolivian species can grow large heads up to 15cm (6in) in diameter, eventually making big clusters. The flowers are borne in a ring around the shoulder of the plant and are usually yellow, more rarely red or orange. The spination is also variable, sometimes fine and dense, but it can be stronger and more open. It has the ability to produce more than one flower from an areole, either at the same time or sequentially. Growth from seed is rapid if given adequate moisture in summer and a bright locality.

REBUTIA NEUMANNIANA

This is the smallest species formerly belonging to the genus weingartia. It grows slowly from seed because it is making a swollen underground root. In its natural habitat, high in the mountains of Bolivia and northern Argentina, the fully grown heads are only 3cm (1in) in diameter. It can grow larger in cultivation, often becoming elongated, and care needs to be taken when re-potting to avoid damaging the sensitive roots. The flowers are produced from the centre of the plant and are orange-yellow or red. A sunny place and less than average watering suits this plant best in cultivation

Similar species: *R. fidaiana*

Rebutia neocummingii *grows large heads that make rings of yellow or orange flowers.*

Rebutia neumanniana *from Argentina has a tuberous root and remains small.*

Stenocactus

A small Mexican genus comprising just a few species, all with many distinctive wavy ribs, except *S. coptonogonus*, which has fewer, straight ribs. The wavy-ribbed species are notoriously difficult to identify and there is little written on the subject to help. When travellers in Mexico encounter specimens of stenocactus, they usually record the plant as 'stenocactus species' and plants or seed are often offered as being from a particular place rather than by name. Even the valid name of the genus has been a matter of much discussion, the alternative name echinofossulocactus still being favoured by some. None of this changes the fact that these are beautiful plants that can be recommended to growers for their attractive spination and flowers, which are produced in abundance in early spring.

Easy to grow, the normal Mexican mix suits them well (see page 45) and in the growing season they enjoy liberal watering and full sun. They are usually raised from seed and it is interesting to observe how the plants are tuberculate when young, only producing the characteristic ribs when they mature.

There are no books that provide a specialist treatment of this genus. The best reference on this subject is an article by Nigel Taylor in the *Cactus and Succulent Journal of Great Britain.*

STENOCACTUS CRISPATUS

This species is the one most often seen in collections although many other names can be found on the labels. It has a large number of wavy ribs and the spines are often long and densely cover the plant. The flowers are white or pink with a darker mid-stripe. It is straightforward to grow from seed and will flower when about 6cm (2.5in) in diameter so long as it has a sunny place in the greenhouse. It will eventually grow offsets and make a cluster of stems.

Similar species: *S. multicostatus*

STENOCACTUS PHYLLACANTHUS

Similar to the previous species but with smaller yellow flowers that are produced sporadically all through the summer. The body remains solitary and the spines are shorter and less dense, the main one being broad and flattened. It requires the same cultivation conditions as *S. crispatus* and is equally easy to raise from seed.

Similar species: *S. vaupelianus*

STENOCACTUS COPTONOGONUS

The most distinct member of the genus, this slow-growing plant has only a few ribs and they are straight and broad. The white flowers, which appear from the centre of the plant, have purple stripes in the petals. Since it always remains solitary, the only way to propagate this plant is from seed, but the young plants are slow and it takes some years before they flower.

ABOVE: Stenocactus crispatus *can be very spiny and usually has striped flowers.*

LEFT: Stenocactus phyllacanthus *from Mexico has small yellow flowers.*

BELOW: Stenocactus coptonogonus *is unusual for the genus in having broad, straight ribs.*

Thelocactus

These plants have many attractions for the collector. The flowers are very beautiful and they are all easy to grow so long as they have a sunny position. Coming from Mexico and neighbouring parts of the USA, they thrive in Mexican mix (see page 45). Easily raised from seed, a few species can grow to great size, sometimes forming large clusters of heads, whilst many will flower while still in small pots. The spination, body form and texture, as well as the wide range of flower colours all combine to reward the grower. The large flowers are produced over several weeks in early summer and can be yellow, white, pink or violet.

A most useful book is *Thelocactus* by John Pilbeam. It describes and illustrates all the species of the genus. There is also a well-illustrated article by A. Mosco and C. Zanovello in the magazine *Cactus & Co.*

THELOCACTUS BICOLOR

This is the most widely distributed species and it has a number of names that have been applied to the various forms found in Mexico and the USA. The one thing they all have in

Thelocactus rinconensis *from Mexico can grow large heads and even clusters.*

common is the large pink flowers, which are among the most beautiful of all cacti. These are readily produced from the young areoles in the centre of the plant throughout the summer months. It is usually raised from seed since the stem, which can grow to 20cm (8in) in height, rarely offsets.

Similar species: *T. heterochromus*

THELOCACTUS RINCONENSIS

A beautiful large species from north-east Mexico that can make solitary heads up to 20cm (8in) in diameter or sometimes large clusters. The flowers are usually white with a sheen to the petals and appear from the centre of the plant. Seedlings are quick growing and often have impressively long spines that can flake apart with age.

Similar species: *T. hexaedrophorus*

THELOCACTUS MACDOWELLII

The glassy white spines of this plant have made it a firm favourite over the years with collectors. The pink flowers look very good against the spines, but it does have a tendency to become rather columnar in a glasshouse, so the sunniest location should be found for this plant. Propagation is always by seed raising since it does not grow offsets unless damaged. It is found naturally in a small area of Nuevo León in Mexico.

Similar species: *T. conothelos*

Thelocactus bicolor *has flowers that are among the most beautiful of all cacti.*

Thelocactus macdowellii, *a Mexican species, is covered with white spines.*

Uebelmannia

In 1966 the cactus hobby was shaken by the arrival in Europe of a few plants of a new species from South America that looked nothing like any known plant. It had been discovered by Leopoldo Horst on rock patches in the forest near Diamentina in Minas Gerais, Brazil and imported by Werner Uebelmann, a Swiss nurseryman. The following year, the Dutch explorer Albert Buining created the new genus uebelmannia into which he placed this plant giving it the name *U. pectinifera*. He also included a plant long known as *Parodia gummifera* that grew in the same area of Brazil but in white quartzite sand. More uebelmannias have subsequently been discovered, all related to one or other of the original species.

Since they became available, these plants have remained highly prized by collectors but they are not beginners' plants. It took some time to ascertain their cultural requirements and even today they remain a challenge to grow well. The key is temperature, at least 15°C (59°F) in winter when they should occasionally be lightly watered. The soil needs to be very open and acidic, so extra grit should be added to the standard mix.

Grafting is often employed for the propagation and culture of uebelmannias but so long as adequate temperatures can be maintained, the relatives of *U. pectinifera* grow well on their own roots. The flowers of this group are very small, yellowish and appear early in the year, those of the *U. gummifera* group are larger and a brighter yellow. This latter group is more difficult to cultivate and few growers succeed in keeping plants on their own roots for long.

The only book dedicated to these plants is the well-illustrated *Uebelmannia and Their Environment* by Rudolf Schulz and Marlon Machado.

UEBELMANNIA PECTINIFERA

This remarkable plant remains solitary and when fully grown can reach over 30cm (12in) in height but such large specimens are rarely seen in cultivation. Its unique appearance and difficulty of cultivation make it very popular with collectors, but most specimens are grafted in order to make cultivation more straightforward. It must be grown from seed, which is not difficult so long as adequate temperature and moisture are provided. The seedlings are often grafted on to pereskiopsis or hylocereus stock when only a few days old. The young plant has a dark purple body that is retained for many years. In habitat, the environmental conditions cause the dark colour to be overlaid by a silvery-white coating of wax that is only present to a lesser degree on older plants in cultivation. The ribs are an almost continuous line of woolly areoles from which the pectinate black spines protrude. They produce their small yellow flowers near the centre in winter or early spring and some water on bright days in winter

Uebelmannia pectinifera is a choice species from Brazil much prized by collectors.

appears to encourage this. In the subspecies *U. pectinifera flavispina*, the body is a bright green and the spines are yellow. This is the easiest form to flower.

UEBELMANNIA GUMMIFERA

This species has been known for many years, having originally been described as *Parodia gummifera* as long ago as 1949. It grows only in patches of white quartzite sand in Minas Gerais, Brazil. Perhaps it is because of its specific pref-

erence for this environment that it is so difficult to cultivate. However, if it is grafted then it becomes possible to have a plant in your collection for many years. It has yellow flowers, larger than those of *U. pectinifera*, and more freely produced in cultivation. The plant remains solitary unless damaged, so propagation must be from seed. It is interesting to observe in habitat that the seeds germinate below the surface layer of sand and develop under the protection of the translucent granules, only emerging into the open when about a centimetre across.

Similar species: *U. buiningii*

Uebelmannia gummifera *ssp.* meninensis *growing in quartzite sand in Minas Gerais, Brazil.*

5 Which Species to Choose – Succulents

Agavaceae (Century Plants)

This family of monocotyledons includes many genera, the best known and most widely grown being agave itself. The rosettes of succulent leaves are often fibrous, a feature that has resulted in extensive planting of *A. sisalana* for the extraction of its fibre to make sisal rope. The sap of some other species is used to make alcoholic drinks such as pulque, mescal and tequila. In some parts of the world, cultivation of the species is of considerable economic importance. There is, however, an unfortunate side effect. The plants thrive in areas where endemic succulents are found and these have often been cleared to make way for plantations of agaves; in Madagascar, for example, the native forests of *Didiereaceae* have suffered extensive damage. Because some agaves are naturally invasive, they are prone to 'escape' from cultivation and spread into the nearby habitats of native succulents that are unable to compete with the more robust species. This is often seen where agaves have been planted as field boundaries.

The rosette diameters of different agave species vary considerably from miniatures of just 15cm (6in) to monsters more than 5m (16ft) in diameter. The succulent leaves are tough and tapering, some with attractive margins, most with fierce spikes on the ends. They are propagated by seeds and also from offsets that some species readily produce, which are usually the reason for their invasive nature, resulting in huge impenetrable clumps. The flowers are spectacular tall spikes

Agave parasana sending up its fast-growing flower stalk.

and result in the death of the rosette that produced them. After a number of years a terminal flower stalk, which can be over 10m (33ft) in height, grows from the centre of the plant at a remarkable speed and produces thousands of flowers. They are called century plants because of the erroneous belief that it takes 100 years to bloom, whereas in reality the time can be anything from about ten to seventy years depending on the species and its circumstances. As well as copious amounts of seed, the flowering rosette may produce offsets at its base or small plantlets on the inflorescence to ensure its survival.

Some species are reasonably hardy and can be grown outdoors with great architectural effect in many parts of the world. The main difficulty in northern Europe is the risk of water collecting in the crown and causing rot. Container-grown specimens add an

Part of the inflorescence of Agave filifera, *which can grow to a height to a height of 2m (6.5ft).*

exotic feel to patio plantings in summer and can be over-wintered in a cold glasshouse where they should be kept dry. The most popular species for this use is *A. americana*, which has a number of attractive variegated forms such as *A. americana marginata* with yellow edges to the leaves, and *A. americana medio-picta*, a very attractively shaped form with a broad white band down the middle of the leaf.

Agaves are native to the New World with the greatest number of species occurring in Mexico. They can also be found naturally in the Caribbean region and the south-western states of the USA. They were among the first succulents to be sent to Europe from the Americas in the middle of the sixteenth century and caused quite a sensation when the flowers were first observed in cultivation.

Among the many other succulent members of the family, the most commonly cultivated are yucca, draceana (dragon tree), and beaucarnea. All these are drought resisting but not as succulent as agaves. They are very suitable for landscaping in warmer climates where most are capable of growing to an imposing size. Some yuccas are completely frost hardy and there are a number that can be successfully grown outside in northern Europe, the variegated cultivars

The tall flower stalk of Agave utahensis kaibabensis *towers above the author's wife.*

being particularly popular. Yuccas have spectacular flowering shoots that bear large numbers of attractive, white bell-shaped flowers. Unlike agaves, the rosette continues to grow and eventually forms a substantial trunk that is often branched.

Finally, there are sansevierias, including the once popular 'Mother-in-law's tongue', *S. trifasciata*, which was guaranteed to survive years of neglect on the lounge window-sill and produce its small, sticky, scented flowers notwithstanding. The variegated form with yellow margins to the leaves used to be particularly favoured. Today, the genus is enjoying something of a revival with more species available and many attractive variegates, some very slow growing. Although they will tolerate shade, the best results are obtained in a bright location where the temperature does not fall below 10°C (50°F). All sansevierias come from southern and eastern Africa.

The best book on the subject is *Agaves, Yuccas and Related Plants* by Mary and Gary Irish. For sansevierias, a useful reference is *Sansevieria Trifasciata Varieties* by B. Juan Chahinian and there is even a specialist group for enthusiasts, the International Sansevieria Society.

AGAVE VICTORIA-REGINAE

One of the best of the Mexican agaves for a small glasshouse and very popular with growers, this easily grown species is usually raised from seed, although young plants will occasionally make offsets. The shape and markings on the leaves vary a lot between individuals, a good specimen will have clear markings and an almost globular rosette. It will flower after many years with an unbranched stalk.

AGAVE UTAHENSIS NEVADENSIS

This is one of a number of forms of this small-growing species from the USA, all of which are among the hardiest of all agaves. If you leave it outside in a British winter, it will survive the cold but not the wet, so plant it on a slope so that the water runs out of the rot-sensitive crown. The flower stalk is unbranched and remarkably tall for the size of the plant.

AGAVE PARVIFLORA

Here is another true miniature and one that can be expected to flower in cultivation when only 15cm (6in) in diameter. The flower stalk is little more than 1m (3ft) tall and usually produces bulbils on the stem that can be used to perpetuate the clone. Offsets are normally produced around the base and these can also be used to propagate more plants. There are a number of other similar looking species but they are bigger growing and consequently need to be larger before they flower.

TOP: Agave victoria-reginae *is a slow-growing, choice species.*

ABOVE: Agave utahensis nevadensis, *a small, hardy species that is a good pot plant.*

Agave parviflora, *planted in a 13cm (5in) pot, just sending up a flower shoot.*

BELOW: Yucca rostrata, *a good plant for landscape gardens, with its spectacular tall inflorescences.*

Agave potatorum, *a large species showing imprints from adjacent leaves.*

AGAVE POTATORUM

The larger agaves make spectacular specimens and this one is a good example. The spectacularly toothed blue leaves make this, and its miniature forms, very popular with collectors who can give it the space it needs. Like many other species, the outline of the teeth are imprinted on to the adjacent leaves when they are tightly wrapped together so that when they unfurl the pattern remains.

YUCCA ROSTRATA

A beautiful species, capable of growing into a tree, it is often cultivated in containers that spend the summer outside but are placed in a cold greenhouse over winter for protection against excess water. Large imported specimens are sometimes available at garden centres and may be expected to flower when they have become established, although not every year.

SANSEVIERIA CV. 'GOLDEN HAHNII'

This is a cultivated selection from the miniature form of *S. trifasciata*. It makes an ideal plant for the window-sill where it enjoys the warm, shady environment and slowly grows into a cluster of rosettes.

Sansevieria *'Golden Hahnii' is a good variegated form for a window-sill.*

Sansevieria pinguicula *is a slow-growing, choice species much prized by collectors.*

Asclepiadaceae (Carrion Flowers and Wax Plants)

This is a family of more than 100 genera, only a few of which include succulent species of interest to the average grower. Most are tropical and many present a challenge in cultivation, a factor that adds to their appeal for the more experienced collector. The most frequently seen representatives include the stapeliads (carrion flowers), ceropegia, hoya (wax plants), and a few caudiciform succulents such as fockea and raphionacme.

The many species of stapeliads undergo regular re-classification under various genera, so the species mentioned here may be found elsewhere with other names. Stapeliads are all stem succulents comprising clumps of thick, soft branches with ribs or tubercles. The flowers are unusual, even spectacular, comprising five petals and varying in size from tiny to 25cm (10in) in diameter. The varied shapes and markings of the flowers are the main attraction of these plants and, although many are easy to grow, some are near impossible to keep alive.

The pollination mechanism is very complex and evolved for specific insects, so that even with several plants flowering at the same time it can be very difficult to set seed. For the determined propagator there are micro-techniques for pollination that can be employed but taking cuttings is the usual method of multiplication. Occasionally, a flower will set without any apparent reason, the result being a pair of elongated fruits, often called 'seed horns', which split to release the seeds, each with a bunch of hairs to facilitate wind dispersal.

The main difficulty in cultivation is their tendency to succumb to fungal attack, causing the stems to rot. As soon as this is seen, often as black patches on the stems, it is necessary to cut away the damaged tissue and treat the cut surfaces with sulphur. Even if only a few stem pieces remain they can be rooted by laying the side of the stem on a rooting medium. Roots are usually formed more effectively from the sides of the stem rather than the cut surface, which is best left above the soil.

Ceropegias have evolved various different body forms. Many have twining stems or ones that scramble on the ground and through trees. These stems may grow from an underground caudex or a number of tubers. Then there are the species with stick-like stems found only on the Canary Islands and a few others with curiously shaped succulent stems. The strange flowers are very diverse but usually look like tiny lanterns with the five corolla lobes fused at their tips. As with stapeliads, the pollination mechanism is complex and fruits are rarely set in cultivation. The twining species tend to become untidy and need to be regularly trained on a trellis and occasionally pruned to keep them in check.

Stapelia grandiflora *can have very large flowers with an unpleasant smell.* Photo: John Pilbeam

Stapelia flavopurpurea *is one of many species suitable for a small pot.* Photo: Tom Jenkins

Stapelia

The oldest name, which once contained all the known species, there are now around forty taxa in this genus that comes from arid areas of southern Africa. The inflorescence is always pubescent and the flowers can be very large in some species. The four-angled stems are usually small but some can grow as high as 1m (3ft).

Huernia

The small stems of this genus make clusters from which the flowers appear on short stalks near to soil level. There are about forty species, some of which have a very prominent annulus in the flower, known colloquially as a 'lifebuoy'. It is widely distributed in Africa and the Arabian peninsular and is the largest genus in the tribe *Stapelieae*.

ABOVE Huernia clavigera, *a small-stemmed species, which grows and flowers easily.*

Huernia zebrina *has flowers of the so-called 'lifebuoy' type.* Photo: Tom Jenkins

Quaqua

A genus recently reinstated for a number of taxa b[…] known as carallumas, it now contains about tw[…] species from southern Africa. They have thin stems [...] small flowers, usually borne on the upper half of the s[…]

Quaqua mammillaris *has small flowers in clusters near the tops of its tuberculate stems.*

Orbea

This is another old name that has recently been reinstated to include plants formerly in other genera, mainly stapelia. The small tuberculate stems make clusters and the attractive flowers are produced from near the ground. They are medium sized and have a prominent annulus. In the case of *O. ciliata* the lobes are fringed with fine hairs that move in the slightest breeze.

Tavaresia

The stems of this fascinating genus are particularly attractive with their many ribs and neat spines on the tubercles, but the main attraction is the remarkable flowers that lie on the ground or hang down like trumpets and can be 7cm (2.75in) in length. There are only two similar species.

ABOVE: Tavaresia barklyi *is a choice species with remarkable large flowers like a trumpet.*

LEFT: Orbea ciliata *has the typical five-lobed flowers of stapeliads, but with a fringe of fine hairs.*
Photo: Tom Jenkins

143

Frerea indica *has the largest persistent leaves of all the stapeliads.*

Piaranthus geminatus *has small prostrate stems and tiny flowers.* Photo: Tom Jenkins

Piaranthus

Here is a genus of dwarf plants from South Africa that make flat clusters of small stems that lie on the ground like mats. The little flowers are freely produced, sometimes in clusters, and the short stems are easy to root and grow on as propagations.

Tromotriche aperta *has short neat stems and flowers on long stalks.*

Tromotriche

A recently expanded genus that now includes plants of diverse appearance including some where the flowers have a long stalk as shown in the illustration of *T. aperta*, which comes from southern Africa.

FREREA INDICA

There are a number of succulents from India but few are seen in cultivation. Perhaps the most popular is this very individual plant, which has the largest leaves in the tribe *Stapelieae*. It is easy to grow but must be kept warm in winter even though the leaves will fall off when the plant is kept dry. It can sometimes be seen labelled as *Caralluma frerei*.

Hoodia

Among the largest of the stapeliads, the stems of this genus can grow to 1m (3ft) tall. The spiny stems of the section hoodia such as *H. gordonii* flower near the tips with large showy flowers that look like papery saucers. The plants in the section trichocaulon such as *H. triebneri* have very similar looking stems but small flowers borne on the sides of the upper half.

Larryleachia

This genus was set up recently to accommodate the species formally known as trichocaulons that do not have spiny stems. Probably the most popular of all stapeliads, they have smooth fat stems and freely produced small flowers. Less than average water and a sunny location are essential and in winter a minimum temperature of 10°C (50°F) and a little water will prevent excess shrivelling.

Larryleachia picta *is a popular plant with flowers only 5mm (0.2in) across.*

ABOVE Hoodia gordonii *with its large papery flowers borne near the top of the stems.*

Ceropegia

These are mainly twining plants that tend to get untidy in the greenhouse if not regularly trained or pruned. Their curious flowers are the main attraction and can be borne in large numbers throughout the growing season. Their large habitat ranges from the Canary Islands, where species have stick-like stems, to India, and many are difficult to cultivate. Some, such as *C. woodii*, have a swollen caudex from which the stems emerge. The root tubers of this easily grown species are used as a grafting stock for difficult stapeliads.

Hoodia triebneri *looks like other hoodias but the flowers are small.*

Ceropegia saundersii *grows long trailing stems that clamber through shrubs.* Photo: John Pilbeam

145

Ceropegia
succulentum *with its
intricate flowers needs
a warm and shady
environment.* Photo:
Tom Jenkins

Brachystelma

Closely related to ceropegia, plants in this genus usually grow a caudex just below the ground from which non-succulent stems grow in the wet season. Some species have long stems on which the small flowers grow, whilst others have short shoots and the evil-smelling flowers appear before the leaves. They come from southern Africa and are usually grown from imported tubers that may appear to establish but have a habit of dying suddenly, perhaps because of incorrect watering or insufficient heat.

Brachystelma
barberae *grows its
evil-smelling flowers
before its leaves.*

Hoya carnosa *is a good climber for a heated
conservatory.* Photo: Tom Jenkins

Hoya

Not all the species of this genus of trailing or climbing shrubs are succulent. They have interesting waxy flowers in large clusters, often produced repeatedly from the same shoots. In culture they require a warm, humid and shady place, so they are not well suited to the succulent glasshouse. Native to the tropical regions of Thailand, Malaysia, India and China.

Crassulaceae (Stonecrops)

This is one of the largest families of succulents with species adapted to live in a wide range of environments including the cold and wet of northern Europe. It is possible to grow some in the garden whereas others will need much care and the protection of a heated glasshouse to thrive. The genera most frequently encountered are crassula, tylecodon, kalanchoe, adromischus, dudleya, echeveria, aeonium, sedum and sempervivum.

Crassula includes species suitable for the garden as well as drought-adapted ones from the deserts of South Africa that are much prized by collectors. The variety of form, ease of cultivation and winter flowering of many species makes this genus particularly popular among growers in Europe. A number of cultivars and hybrids are also available. To maintain the more rampant growers in a neat condition, it

Crassula mesembryanthemopsis, *a choice species that is a very popular choice for shows.* Photo: Tom Jenkins

is necessary to prune them occasionally and even start new cuttings to avoid them getting overgrown.

Kalanchoe are mainly tropical and require higher temperatures in cultivation, many becoming too large for the average glasshouse. They have attractive leaves and hybrids of the small *K. blossfeldiana* with their large range of flower colours have become common houseplants. A few species propagate themselves very successfully by dropping adventitious buds from the leaf margins that quickly spread around the glasshouse. They have already become a weed in areas of the world with a suitable climate, such as parts of South America.

A recent fashion in succulent plants has favoured adromischus, a genus of small, easily grown plants from South Africa. They have attractive leaves and make neat plants in small pots. They are readily propagated by rooting leaves, so enthusiasts can exchange clones among themselves without difficulty.

Dudleyas are also very popular with collectors for their leaves, which are often covered in a white powdery coating. They come from Mexico and California where they receive winter rainfall and they retain this winter growing preference in cultivation. Great care has to be taken to avoid touching the leaves since rub marks are permanent.

Similar in appearance to dudleyes, echeverias were once more popular than they are today but their large rosettes of variously coloured leaves can make a spectacular display and it is only a matter of time before their popularity returns. There are many hybrids that extend the flower-ing season or accentuate particular characteristics of the leaves. A few species are nearly hardy and are used in summer bedding schemes in cooler climates, like in Britain, where they are a common feature of floral clocks and lettering.

Many sedums and sempervivums may be grown outdoors where they can withstand some frost in winter, especially if given a well-drained soil and sunny position. They are popular with alpine gardeners and many attractive hybrids are available. After a sempervivum rosette flowers it will die but the freely offsetting habit will ensure its continuity. For the glasshouse succulent collector, a number of tender sedums have attractive leaves and star-like flowers. The related genus aeonium from the Canary Islands usually has its rosette of leaves on a branched stem and, like sempervivum, its flowers are terminal. With unbranched species that means it is necessary to start new plants from seed.

Crassula

A large genus of nearly 300 species but few are popular in cultivation since they tend to be untidy and grow rampantly. The species available for the succulent enthusiast are generally neat growers and make compact, low plants that usually flower freely in the winter months, a particular benefit at a time when there can be a shortage of flowers. Propagation from cuttings is straightforward but the need to water gently in winter can cause fungal problems, so an occasional treatment with a fungicide is a wise precaution.

Crassula argentea *'Hummel's Sunset' needs a sunny place to develop its best colours.*

Crassula comptonii *flowering in the winter.* Photo: Tom Jenkins

A very popular species that makes a neat tree-shaped bush with thick stems and succulent round leaves is *C. argentea*, the 'money plant'. It needs good light to keep its neat habit, especially the variegated form 'Hummel's Sunset'.

Tylecodon

A genus of about forty-five species from southern Africa that includes large shrubs and tiny plants, the latter being very suitable for cultivation in pots. They come from the winter rainfall area and retain the desire to grow in our winter so should be watered in autumn through to early spring, during which time they will leaf and flower. A shady place in summer, when they should be kept dry, is ideal. The thickened stems that grow into attractive shapes are the main attribute of these interesting miniature plants.

Tylecodon buchholzianus *flowers in winter when it needs to be lightly watered.* Photo: Tom Jenkins

Kalanchoe

This very widespread genus can be found in Africa, Asia and even the Americas. In cultivation they tend to grow in the winter and flower in spring. Some species have attractive velvety leaves and can become very large. Most are easy to root from cuttings and some, like *K. dagremontianum*, produce young plants along the margins of the leaves that fall to the ground and grow, a real problem in a glasshouse where it is prone to becoming a weed. The bell-shaped flowers are generally carried on a tall stalk but not reliably produced on all species in cultivation.

Kalanchoe pumila *will grow and flower easily in a bright place.* Photo: John Pilbeam

Kalanchoe tomentosa *from Madagascar has pretty markings on its velvety leaves.*

Kalanchoe dagremontianum *can become invasive through plantlets falling from its leaf margins.*

Adromischus

Popularity for this genus has never been greater and specialist collections of the many forms of the twenty or so species can often be seen. Propagation is generally easy from leaves and many have been brought back from habitat in recent years so that the true variability of the species can be appreciated. The flowers are fairly insignificant, being borne on a narrow spike; it is the leaf shape, colour and arrangement that delight the grower.

Dudleya

In their native homeland of Mexico and California these plants make impressive clusters of rosettes on rocky places, often near the sea. The leaves are usually covered with a white waxy coating that easily rubs off and permanently marks the leaves, so they are particularly difficult to transport to shows. They are similar in appearance to echeverias but differ in their flowers, and their need to grow in the winter,

Adromischus marianiae *is a very variable species of this popular genus.*

RIGHT: Adromischus
trigynus *can easily be
propagated by rooting
leaves.*

BELOW: Adromischus
marianiae fa. herrei
*is easy to grow but
difficult to find for
sale.*

BOTTOM: Dudleya
greenii *is a pretty
miniature from Baja,
California.* Photo:
John Pilbeam

Dudleya pachyphytum *is a slow-growing, choice
species that is rare in collections.*

as they would during the rainy season in habitat. They are regarded as choice plants in cultivation and present no particular problem to grow so long as they are watered in autumn and a little in winter.

Echeveria

Although not as popular as they once were, these plants have attractive rosettes of colourful leaves and attractive flowers. There are also many easily grown hybrids that have been bred both for the leaves and some for the flowers. They are native to Mexico, the USA and parts of South America. Most can be propagated from leaves, but a few species are best raised from seed or from stem cuttings. The dead leaves around the bottom of the plant provide a hiding place for pests, so regular attention to cleanliness is essential to get a perfect plant. Probably the most beautiful species is *E. laui*, which was only found a few years ago in Mexico. Unfortunately, it is also one of the most difficult to grow and should be carefully watered and given a sunny place in the greenhouse.

Echeveria lindsayana *is often seen at shows and can be propagated by rooting leaves.*

Echeveria setosa *makes clusters of heads with hairy leaves, here starting to flower.*

Graptopetalum

Another small genus of rosette-forming plants from Mexico that resembles echeveria except for their flowers. This resemblance is particularly striking in *G. suaveolens*, which was transferred to this genus from sedum. The best species is *G. bellum*, which was described as a new genus – tacitus – following its discovery in 1972, but was subsequently renamed.

Echeveria laui *is a beautiful species but tricky to grow well.*

Graptopetalum suaveolens *looks like an echeveria but has very different flowers.*

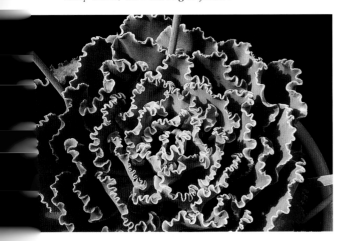

Echeveria 'Blue Curl' *is a popular hybrid with large rosettes.*

Aeonium arboreum *'Schwarzkopf'is a good plant for a conservatory and can be put outside in summer.*

Graptopetalum bellum *'Super Star' is a darker-flowering selection of the species.*

Aeonium

Most of this genus are native to the Canary Islands. The rosettes are sometimes close to the ground but often grow at the top of a long, branching stem. Some species are monocarpic, which means that the flowering rosette dies, but there are usually offsets to grow on. The variously coloured flowers appear on a large multi-branched flower stalk and can be very spectacular. The dark purple leaves of the cultivar A. *arboreum* 'Schwarzkopf' make it a popular indoor plant that can be put in the garden in summer.

Sedum

A large genus of several hundred species, only a few of which are a challenge to grow. Many are hardy and can be grown outside in a rockery or sink garden all through the year. The flowers, which are readily produced, are white, yellow or pink.

Sempervivum

Most of these plants are from Europe and are completely hardy outside if grown in a well-drained medium, so avoiding waterlogging. The rosettes are monocarpic but offsets are always produced and large clumps of stems will eventually be formed. There are many hybrids and prop-

Sedum hernandezii, *only recently described, is a choice species from Mexico.* Photo: John Pilbeam

Sempervivum tectorum is one of the best succulents to grow outside all the year round.

With species to appeal to beginners as well as the more advanced collector, euphorbia is among the most popular of all genera in succulent collections. Some are easy to grow, whilst others are a real challenge even to the most experienced cultivator. A number of the choicest species have a caudex that would be underground in habitat but in culture is best grown on top of the soil to reduce the risk of rotting. Particularly fashionable are the species from Madagascar, many of which have very ornamental leaves but need more warmth in cultivation to flourish. Also from Madagascar is *E. millii*, 'Crown of Thorns', which is often grown as a houseplant and responds well to windowsill culture. It flowers almost perpetually so long as it is kept warm and watered. As with other euphorbias, the bright colour of the flower comes from coloured bracts rather than petals.

agation is very easy by rooting heads. They are known as 'houseleeks' because of their propensity to grow on the roofs of houses and they are probably popular because it is possible to make a collection outdoors in a sink garden or rockery.

Euphorbiaceae (Spurges)

Of the thousands of species in this family, the collector will principally be interested in the succulent members of the genera euphorbia and monadenium. Even to those growers who prefer cacti, euphorbia has a number of species that will appeal, if only because they look so much like cacti. In fact the genus euphorbia has evolved a splendid diversity of stem succulence that gives the specialist collector the opportunity to amass a collection of species with very different appearances all from this one genus. A feature common to almost all is the stem latex, which has a milky appearance and can be toxic or at least irritating, requiring care in handling to avoid introducing it into eyes or other sensitive body parts. Most species will produce flowers of both sexes even if not at the same time, whilst others are dioecious, which means that an individual only produces male or female flowers. The flowers are small but can be produced in large numbers, sometimes with prominent, brightly coloured bracts around them.

Euphorbia ingens can become a huge tree in Africa, its natural habitat. Photo: Daphne Pritchard

Monadeniums are tropical and require considerable warmth to thrive. They are better suited to the more advanced collector but their spectacular appearance make the extra cultural effort worthwhile.

The succulent members of this family have been wonderfully described and illustrated in *The Euphorbia Journal*, a set of ten books for the serious addict.

EUPHORBIA INGENS

This is the giant of the genus and grows into a huge tree up to 10m (33ft) in height with multiple branching. It can be the dominant plant in the landscape and occurs over a vast area of Africa. In cultivation it can also grow at an alarming pace, particularly if it has a free root run. It is very architectural and frequently used for plantings in large buildings and shopping centres where many observers would mistake it for a cactus.

Euphorbia trigona *has patterned stems and deciduous leaves on the new growth.*

Euphorbia ingens *grows quickly in cultivation and is often used in exotic indoor landscapes.*

EUPHORBIA COOPERI

Another widespread species in the tropical parts of Africa, it makes a tree up to 5m (16ft) in height with a central stem and candelabra branches constricted into segments that are wider at the lower part. The lower branches are later deciduous leaving a clear trunk. The latex of this species is particularly poisonous

EUPHORBIA GORGONIS

This is a small-growing species of the 'medusa head' type of euphorbia. The thick central stem has a series of short arms arranged around the broad head. It is a choice species, much prized by collectors because of its symmetrical form and neat habit. It comes from the Eastern Cape region of South Africa where it grows almost flush with the ground.

Euphorbia cooperi *growing in its natural habitat in Kenya.* Photo: Daphne Pritchard

FAR LEFT: Euphorbia gorgonis *is one of the best of the 'medusa head' type euphorbias.*

EUPHORBIA ENOPLA

One of a number of similar-looking species, this easily grown plant makes an attractive branched specimen with its prominent, red thorny peduncles that are derived from the dried flowers stalks. It is an example of a commonly grown, bush-forming species from Cape Province, South Africa.

Euphorbia enopla *has prominent red peduncles left over after flowering.*

Euphorbia
quadrangularis *has
marbled stems and
small yellow flowers.*
Photo: Tom Jenkins

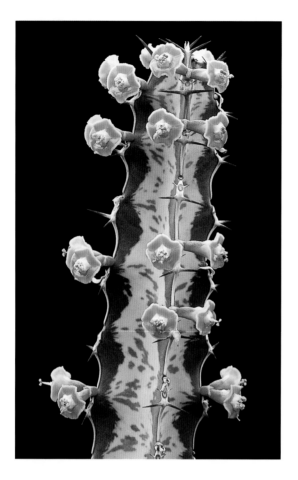

Euphorbia horrida striata *has white stems and
green stripes.*

EUPHORBIA QUADRANGULARIS

A sparsely branched plant from Tanzania that
can grow to over 2m (6.5ft) in height. It has an
interesting marbled pattern on its four-angled
stems and bright yellow flowers. Said to be difficult to cultivate, it needs to be kept above
10°C (50°F) in winter and watered with care.
Propagation is achieved by cuttings, which can
be readily rooted.

EUPHORBIA HORRIDA STRIATA

Euphorbia horrida is a very popular plant with
many forms, some can grow tall whilst other
make neat clusters of almost globular stems. This
form is outstanding for its almost white bodies
that can be prominently striped, as in the illustrated specimen. It is known from a wild population in South Africa and is one of the most
cactus-like of euphorbias. Very easy to grow in
a bright place, it will eventually form a sizeable
cluster of stems. The flowers are dioecious.

EUPHORBIA MELOFORMIS

Even those who only have a few euphorbias are
likely to grow this outstanding plant. It remains
depressed globular, making a clump of shiny
green stems with persistent peduncles left
behind following flowering. Male and female
flowers are produced on different individuals so
you need a pair to set seeds, which are easily
raised. It can be found naturally occurring in
South Africa near to the similar *E. valida*.

Euphorbia meloformis *remains globular and
makes large clumps of stems.*

156

EUPHORBIA OBESA

Perhaps the ultimate succulent, this solitary-stemmed species is the most popular of all euphorbias. Its appealing shape and markings, together with its ease of culture make it irresistible to growers. Plants are either male or female and only very rarely both, so the typical euphorbia fruits with three seeds can only be produced if you have two plants of different sexes. When ripe, like all euphorbias, the pods explode and project the seeds some distance, so they can often be found growing in the pots of their neighbours on the greenhouse bench. Another South African species, it is now protected from illegal collecting, which was a major threat to this unique plant since it has such a limited distribution.

The male flowers of Euphorbia obesa.

The female flowers of Euphorbia obesa *developing into typical euphorbia fruits with three seeds.*

Euphorbia obesa *is among the most popular of all succulents.*

EUPHORBIA STELLATA

Another popular and commonly available species, *E. stellata* has a swollen root that would be underground in habitat but in cultivation is usually raised above the ground to reduce the risk of rotting. The flattened stems can become long in age and may need pruning to keep them tidy. This is an easy plant to grow, as is the similar *E. squarrosa*, both coming from South Africa.

Euphorbia stellata *has a large swollen root that is underground in habitat.*

Euphorbia bupleurifolia *is a slow-growing species which is sought after by collectors.*

EUPHORBIA BUPLEURIFOLIA

The pineapple-like stem of this distinctive species is topped by a crown of non-succulent leaves and can grow to a height of 20cm (8in) with age. During the dry season, the leaves fall and then the flowers, which are dioecious, are produced just before the leaves grow again in spring. This choice species is much sought after by collectors and, although seedlings are easy to raise, they are only occasionally available for sale. It usually remains solitary but branches are occasionally produced, which makes the plant even more appealing.

Euphorbia ankarensis *is a Madagascan species which flowers before it grows its leaves.* Photo: Tom Jenkins

EUPHORBIA ANKARENSIS

Like all the other species from Madagascar, this plant needs a temperature of at least 10°C (50°F) in winter and will do better if kept even warmer. An occasional light watering in winter will prevent excess dehydration. This species has a sparsely branched, smooth trunk that can grow to 20cm (8in) in height with a crown of deciduous hairy leaves at the top. The flowers are borne at the end of the bare stem in early spring, followed by the leaves. Very similar, but easier to grow is *E. millotii*, which is freely branching and can be propagated by rooting cuttings of the branches.

EUPHORBIA CYLINDRIFOLIA

One of the most popular of the Madagascan species, the seedlings form a swollen stem from which long arms grow. These are held horizontally just above the ground and end in a cluster of small, grooved leaves. A warm and shady place with plenty of water in summer and a minimum temperature of 15°C (59F) in winter suits this easy plant. The branches can be rooted but they do not form a caudex. The similar *E. francoisii* grows a bigger caudex and has shorter branches, the leaves being larger and often beautifully marked, particularly in young plants.

ABOVE Euphorbia cylindrifolia *from Madagascar slowly makes a caudex.*

Euphorbia milli *will flower outside throughout the summer.*

Euphorbia millotii *soon grows into an impressive cluster of stems.* Photo: Tom Jenkins

Euphorbia francoisii *has forms with very colourful leaves.*

Euphorbia millii *hybrids are now available with much larger flowers.*

EUPHORBIA MILLII

The so-called 'Crown of Thorns' is a popular houseplant and thrives on a bright window-sill. It can be put outside in summer where it will flower continuously with red or sometimes yellow blooms. Easily rooted from stem cuttings, this plant needs to be kept warm in winter and will retain its leaves so long as it has moisture at the root. A number of hybrids with larger flowers have been introduced recently from the Far East and can sometimes be found in garden centres.

Monadenium

Although most of the thirty species of monadenium cannot be recommended for the average grower because of the difficulty of cultivation, a few are fairly easy so long as they are kept warm. *M. rubellum* is one of the most attractive with its caudex and pink flowers. Cuttings of the stems will root and produce a caudex, so making this miniature species easy to propagate.

Monadenium rubellum *easily grows into a colourful plant if kept warm.* Photo: Tom Jenkins

Liliaceae (Lilies)

Another large family of monocotyledons (see Appendix IV) with more than 3,000 species, only a few hundred of which are succulent. The main genera of interest here are aloe, gasteria and haworthia, all from the Old World, principally Africa. These popular plants make attractive rosettes of succulent leaves ranging in size from miniatures a few inches across to plants such as the tree aloes that can grow up to 20m (65.5ft) tall. This tree form of growth is remarkable for a moncotyledon since they do not make the solid wood found in dicotyledons, but rather a light but strong fibrous structure that has to support the weight of the heavy crown of succulent leaves.

Like agaves, with which they are often confused, aloes are popular landscape plants in suitably warm climates and many hybrids have been produced to increase their vigour and floriferousness. Unlike agaves, their flowers are borne laterally and the shoot continues to grow after flowering. The flowers are tubular, brightly coloured and often hang down for the pollina-

tors, which are usually sunbirds, the African equivalent of humming-birds, or bees. Most in demand for glasshouse culture are the miniatures of the genus such as *A. haworthioides* and *A. descoingsii*, two examples of the many from Madagascar. There are also small-growing hybrids of these and others that make excellent pot plants and can usually be propagated from offsets.

Most aloes are easy to cultivate, the main exception being the dwarf 'grass aloes' that are a real challenge to grow. Some species retain their winter growing period in the northern hemisphere and must be watered in our winter for successful cultivation. Although the flowers are particularly welcome in winter, they can look rather dried up during the summer.

Increasingly popular after the publication of an excellent book on the genus, gasterias are easy to grow and include a number of desirable species. Many retain the juvenile characteristic of growing their leaves in a row rather than a rosette, a feature of *G. armstrongii*, which is a slow-growing and sought-after species. The pink

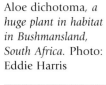

Aloe dichotoma, a huge plant in habitat in Bushmansland, South Africa. Photo: Eddie Harris

flowers are readily produced on long racemes and have a swollen base to the flower tube that gives the genus its name ('gaster' means belly).

Surely the most popular succulent genus at present is haworthia. This is reflected in the proliferation of publications, the high price of the plants and the number of entries in show classes. They are prized for their neat, low-growing rosettes of leaves that are often beautifully patterned or attractively margined. Some have translucent 'windows' in the surface that allow the light to pass into the interior where photosynthesis takes place. In nature, many of these leaves will be buried but in cultivation it is safer to have them exposed to reduce the risk of rot. The flowers are borne on long racemes but all are similar and unexciting so some growers remove the flower stems to retain the neat appearance of the collection.

Haworthias are generally easy to grow but some species are notoriously slow, making them particularly desirable. They repay regular re-potting when the naturally produced dead roots and dead outer leaves can be removed to improve presentation and reduce the risk of rot. Propagation of a particular clone can be achieved by removing and rooting the offsets when available or individual leaves. Seed, freshly sown after collection, is also a good way to get more plants. For this you need two flowering plants of the same species, taking care to cross the young flowers on one raceme with older flowers on the other using a fine brush.

Among the many books about aloes, the recently published *Guide to the Aloes of South Africa* by B-E. van Wyk and G. Smith is very well illustrated and shows what magnificent plants they are in their native habitats. *Gasterias of South Africa* by E. van Jaarsveld is an excellent book on the genus and contains splendid coloured drawings of the plants by E. Ward-Hilhorst. *Haworthia Revisited* by Bruce Bayer is well illustrated and captures the attraction of these remarkable plants.

ALOE DICHOTOMA

One of the tree aloes, this species grows to impressive dimensions in the north-western parts of the Cape area of South Africa where it forms 'forests'. It is locally known as the 'quiver tree', supposedly because the hollowed-out branches were used as quivers. It grows easily and quickly from seed and is often used in landscape gardening where the climate is suitable.

ALOE PILLANSII

Another large-growing tree aloe, this species can also be found in the north-western Cape area of South Africa but it is less extensively distributed and considered endangered, mainly due to over-grazing, which destroys the seedlings. The branches are characteristically erect and fewer in number than *A. dichotoma*. The seedlings grow rather slowly for a plant that will ultimately become so large and are not widely available.

ALOE MARLOTHII

Very widespread in central-east Africa, this single-stemmed species has almost horizontal racemes of erect flowers that distinguish it from other species. It grows easily and quickly from seed and can reach over 4m (13ft) in height in its homeland. It is popular as a landscape plant in places where the climate allows, and will even withstand some frost.

Aloe marlothii *flowering in habitat with its distinctive inflorescence.* Photo: Daphne Pritchard

ALOE ANGELICA

One of the less common aloes in cultivation, this plant comes from the Northern Province of South Africa where it is plentiful in its restricted distribution area. The stems, which are usually solitary, can grow to 4m (13ft) in height and the yellow flowers are borne on tall branched inflorescence.

Aloe angelica in flower in the Northern Province of South Africa. Photo: Daphne Pritchard

Aloe melanacantha becomes very colourful during dry periods in habitat. Photo: Tom Jenkins

ALOE MELANACANTHA

This is a more manageable size for cultivation and is popular with growers due to its attractive rosettes with black thorns. In habitat the leaves become a wonderful reddish colour in the dry season but this is difficult to achieve in cultivation. It is propagated by seed raising but rarely produces its 1m (3ft) unbranched inflorescence in culture.

ALOE TOMENTOSA

One of the many aloes from the Arabian peninsula, this species is characterized by its pinkish flowers, which are covered in hairs. The inflorescence is well branched and grows to over 1m (3ft) in height. It is easy to cultivate and makes a good landscape plant in warm climates.

ALOE ERINACEA

Following the availability of seed, this plant has become very popular in collections due to its slow-growing rosettes of attractively toothed leaves that colour best in good light. It comes from Namibia and prefers to grow in winter when it should be put in the brightest place

ABOVE Aloe tomentosa *from the Arabian peninsular is a good landscape plant.*

available, lightly watered and kept at a minimum temperature of 10°C (50°F). It tends to become more columnar in cultivation and rarely flowers but is still worth growing for its overall appearance.

Aloe erinacea *is now often seen in collections following seed becoming available.*

Aloe pillansii, *here at Cornel's Kop, is considered an endangered species.* Photo: Tom Jenkins

Aloe vera is famous for the medicinal properties of its sap.

Aloe claviflora in flower showing its characteristic horizontal inflorescence.

ALOE VERA

Perhaps the most famous of all aloes because of its claimed medicinal properties. Much has been written on the subject and garden centres sell thousands of specimens to people wanting to extract the sap from the leaves. It grows easily and has been introduced to places all over the world where it has become naturalized. It is difficult to know where it originally grew wild, but

Aloe vacillans *can have red or sometimes yellow flowers.*

North Africa or the Middle East are possibilities and there is a population on the Maltese islands, which is claimed by the locals to be original. There is a similar plant called *A. vacillans* from Saudi Arabia that can have red or yellow flowers.

ALOE CLAVIFLORA

An interesting and widespread species with asymmetrical rosettes that lie on the ground. The inflorescense grows horizontally just above the ground and when the flowers open, they hang down – presumably to allow birds on the ground to reach up into the flower. It grows easily in cultivation from seed and flowers reliably when a few years old.

Aloe parvula *is a miniature species from Madagascar and flowers in winter.*

ALOE PARVULA

One of a number from Madagascar, this attractive miniature aloe should be watered lightly and given a minimum temperature of 10°C (50°F) in winter, when it grows. The flowers are reliably produced in autumn or winter and add to the appeal of this easily grown plant. This and other small species, such as *A. descoingsii*, have been used to produce many free-flowering hybrids with attractive leaves such as 'White Diamond' illustrated here.

GASTERIA ARMSTRONGII

One of the most popular species of this South African genus, it easily grows into clusters, each head consisting of a number of wide distichous leaves. It can be propagated by removing offsets, which often have their own roots already. The inflorescence can be up to 40cm (16in) in height with typical pink flowers borne sequentially along its length.

GASTERIA ELLAPHIEAE

A recently described small species that is already regarded as choice by collectors due to its slow growth. It is not difficult to cultivate but needs to be given good light to retain its character. It can be propagated by leaf cuttings or from offsets, which are sparingly produced.

ABOVE: Aloe X 'White Diamond', *an example of many small hybrids with nicely pattered leaves.*

LEFT: Gasteria armstrongii, *one of the best species for collectors and the show bench.*

Gasteria elaphieae *is a recently described, small-growing species.*

HAWORTHIA MAUGHANII

H. maughanii has a windowed end to the leaf that allows light to pass to the inside where photosynthesis takes place. The tips of the leaves are flush with the ground in habitat but are best grown higher in cultivation to reduce the risk of rotting. Very similar is *H. truncata*, some clones of which can grow quickly to make big clusters. It has its leaves arranged distichously, a unique feature in haworthia. Both species are extremely popular with collectors and are often seen on the show bench.

Haworthia
maughanii *showing
a flower typical of
the genus.*

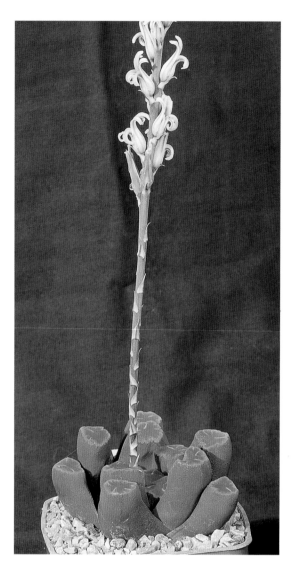

HAWORTHIA CORRECTA

This is one of many species of haworthia with
windowed leaves in a rosette including *H.
emelyae, H. comptoniana, H. bruynsii, H. magnifica* and *H. springbokvlakensis.* They are sometimes difficult to tell apart and many have
very attractive markings on the ends of the
leaves. Selected clones and hybrids are also
available to satisfy the demand from enthusiasts for this popular type. Propagation of
desirable clones is usually done by leaf cuttings since offsets are rarely produced. It
should be given a bright place and regularly
watered in summer and a little in winter as
well. Regular re-potting to remove dead leaves
and roots is a good idea since haworthias
renew their thickened roots regularly.

HAWORTHIA BOLUSII

Also popular with growers are the few species
that have attractive leaves, dried at the tips into
a thatch to protect the plant from sun. In cultivation they require full sun and careful watering to keep their typical appearance. Similar
species are *H. semiviva, H. lockwoodii* and *H.
arachnoidea* and all require care to avoid getting
water between the leaves which could cause rot.

Haworthia truncata *is probably the most popular
species and the most unusual.*

Haworthia correcta *is a window-leafed species
from South Africa.*

Haworthia bolusii *needs plenty of sun to keep it
natural with dried leaf ends.*

Mesembryanthemaceae (Living Stones and Relatives)

This family of succulent plants is almost as large as the family *Cactaceae* with around 2,000 recognized species broken down into more than 100 genera, of which only a few are grown by non-specialist collectors. The family exhibits a remarkable diversity of form and size and has fascinated plant enthusiasts for over 300 years. The majority of species occur naturally in southern Africa with a few found in the Middle East and Australia. Bees are the main pollinators of the day-flowering species that have bright multi-petalled flowers. An interesting feature of the resulting fruits is that they usually have a mechanism that opens when wetted, so dispersing the seeds when favourable germination conditions are present.

Success with growing these highly adapted plants requires the sunniest location available and an understanding of their growing periods, since these are largely retained when brought into culture. The most popular genera for glasshouse culture are the ones containing neat small-growing species, many of which are outstanding mimicry plants. Examples of these are cheiridopsis, conophytum, faucaria, fenestraria, frithia, lithops, nananthus, pleiospilos and titanopsis. Propagation is usually by seed but cuttings taken from clumps of heads are generally easy to root during their growing season. The joy of growing from seed is the diversity you get among the seedlings, so allowing you to choose the best-marked ones whilst having spares to swap with other enthusiasts. Exchanging spare plants or cuttings is one of the best parts of the hobby and mesembryanthemums are well suited to the practice.

One of the best ways to enhance your interest and obtain rarely offered plants is to join a specialist group like the Mesemb Study Group. There are a few books about individual genera such as conophytum or lithops, but the best recent book on the whole family is *Mesembs of the World*. It is very beautifully illustrated and describes all the genera with specific cultural advice and useful references to further reading.

Cheiridopsis

A genus of more than thirty species of diverse appearance, often with consecutive pairs of leaves of different shapes. Some grow into small shrubs while others are dwarf and so are the popular ones to grow in a glasshouse. With some, the old leaves dry to form a sheath around the base of the new pair. They can be elongated in shape, a characteristic associated with the well-known *C. cigarettifera*. The flowers, which are carried on a stalk, are usually yellow but can be white or pinkish. Most are easy to grow and respond well to being watered in autumn and into winter when flowering can be expected.

Cheiridopsis caroli-schmidtii. Photo: John Pilbeam

Cheiridopsis ausensis. Photo: Eddie Harris

Conophytum

Among the most popular genera for glasshouse culture, conophytums make low cushions of small heads or can be solitary, but this is rare. The leaves often have attractive patterns of lines and dots in a range of greens, pinks and browns, sometimes with windows in the top surface. The flowers can be shades of pink, lilac, white or yellow and are often scented. They are not difficult to grow so long as their growing period is observed. They should be watered from about August when the heads will be covered by the

Conophytum pellucidum.

Conophytum wettsteinii.

OPPOSITE PAGE:
Flowering mesembryanthemums at Doringwater Flats, South Africa. Photo: Chris Rodgerson

Conophytum ectypum.

Conophytum concavum.

dried remains of the previous year's leaves. As growth commences, the new leaves will burst through the skins, some heads having split into two new pairs of leaves hence expanding the clump. Flowering will take place later in the autumn or early spring in some species. They should be kept dry from February with very little water in the spring when light shading from sun is advisable.

Conophytum frutescens.

Conophytum taylorianum rosynense.

Fenestraria

These dwarf plants form mats of club-shaped leaves with windowed ends that are buried up to the tips in habitat. It is an outstanding example of how windows in the leaves allow light to pass into the interior of the leaf for photosynthesis, whilst most of the leaf is buried to protect it from excess transpiration. This can also be found in unrelated plants such as haworthia as well as many other mesembryanthemums. Fenestrarias require a sandy soil and should be lightly watered from June to October, and then be kept dry for the rest of the year. They have a tendency to become lush with long leaves if not given a harsh life, but in any case the leaves should not be buried in cultivation. There is only one species, *F. rhopalophylla*, with a long-tubed, white flower and its subspecies *aurantiaca* with a larger yellow flower.

BELOW: Fenestraria rhopalophylla aurantiaca. Photo: Eddie Harris

BOTTOM: Fenestraria rhopalophylla. Photo: John Pilbeam

Faucaria tigrina. Photo: John Pilbeam

Faucaria candida. Photo: Eddie Harris

Faucaria

A popular genus, which has been cultivated for many years because of its interesting appearance. The triangular leaves are usually edged with a row of teeth making the leaf pair look like jaws, hence the name 'tigrina', referring to a tiger's jaws. The small rosettes of leaf pairs cluster to make low clumps that often take on a pinkish hue in strong light. The flowers appear in autumn, they are usually yellow or occasionally white and are easily produced in cultivation. Water sparingly from summer into autumn to keep the plants compact and colourful. Faucarias are good plants for beginners with many similar species to choose from.

Frithia pulchra.

Frithia

Although superficially similar to fenestraria, these plants are summer growers and easily make free-flowering clumps in cultivation. In habitat, like fenestraria, the textured leaf tips are the only part of the plant visible above ground, the windowed ends allowing light to enter. In dry times, the leaves pull down further into the soil for extra protection against transpirational loss. In culture, frithias grow in the summer and should be watered from April until September during which time they will produce their pretty short-tubed purple or white flowers.

Lithops

Without doubt the most famous and popular of the 'stone plants'. Lithops have evolved a remarkable similarity to the stones among which they grow. Each head comprises a pair of fused leaves with a fissure between, their upper surfaces being variously coloured and patterned to blend into their surroundings. Many also have a large window or a number of small ones that allow light into the interior surfaces of the leaf where photosynthesis takes place. During the winter and early spring the leaves dry up to a thin sheath, which covers the newly developing pair or pairs of leaves beneath. After watering, the new leaves swell and break through, the new pair or pairs at right angles to the old. The short-tubed flowers are either yellow or white and often every head will flower to make a spectacular show, sometimes completely obscuring the plant itself.

As well as the normal species, there are a number of sports, selections or forms with unusual and sometimes dramatically different coloured leaves. Some of these occur naturally in wild populations; perhaps the best known being *L. optica rubra*, which has pink-purple leaves rather than the olive green of the normal form.

Lithops are often distributed with Cole numbers, which are references applied by Desmond Cole to populations of plants from which he collected and distributed seeds. He was also the author of a comprehensive book on the genus *Lithops – Flowering Stones*, now out of print and difficult to find. The most recent book about these fascinating plants is *Lithops – Treasures of the Veld* by S. Hammer.

A collection of lithops grown in a pan makes an attractive feature in a collection.

Lithops pseudotruncatella elisabethiae.

ABOVE: Lithops lesliei mariae *in flower.*

Lithops lesliei mariae *in bud.*

Nananthus

These form flat clumps of boat-shaped leaves arranged in a series of pairs to make a rosette, below which are thick tuberous roots. The leaves are often covered with white dots and the yellow flowers are produced in the autumn. Nananthus are easy to grow and should be watered from late summer into winter. There are only a few species that are difficult to distinguish.

FAR RIGHT:
Pleiospilos peersii.
Photo: Eddie Harris

Nananthus transvaalensis. Photo: Eddie Harris

Pleiospilos

A small genus of easily recognized plants with thick, rock-like spotted leaves that are covered with a waxy layer. Some species make solitary heads, each with one or two pairs of large fleshy leaves, whilst others form low clusters. The flowers, which are borne on short stalks, range from yellow to orange in colour, and a number may be produced simultaneously from the same head. They are produced in autumn or winter and have a strong scent, reminiscent of coconuts. Plants should be lightly watered in summer and autumn, when the head of a well-cultivated plant will probably have two pairs of turgid leaves. They are particularly susceptible to damage from red spider mite that scars the leaves (see page 52).

Titanopsis

The remarkable leaves of this genus distinguish it from others in the family with their prominent warts. They make low clusters of rosettes with a thickened rootstock. The ends of the leaves are covered with white, pink, green or brown warts that give the plants a most attractive appearance and account for their popularity. The flowers are usually yellow or a pale amber colour and appear tucked into the centres of the rosettes. They are easy to grow and should be watered from summer into autumn when the flowers appear.

Miscellaneous Succulents

There are plants in many genera that have evolved succulence as a way to survive in places that have a prolonged dry period even though other species in those genera are non-succulent. Also, since succulence is not a precise term, there are borderline cases that may or may not be regarded as succulent depending on your view. One attempt at listing succulent plants can be found in the *BCSS Handbook of Shows*, which lists all the plants eligible as succulents in their shows. The following pages describe, in no particular order, some of the plants that are becoming increasingly popular. It is hoped that this will be of particular interest to those who want to grow something a bit more unusual that does not fit into any of the previous categories.

Many of the plants described and illustrated here can be regarded as caudiciforms, some of which have become much sought after during the last few decades, even taking on cult status in the succulent world. Caudiciform describes plants from many families which survive periods of drought by storing water in a swollen, perennial storage organ known as a caudex. When in growth the plants produce stems and leaves, usually of a non-succulent nature and often with a clambering habit, from the caudex.

Caudiciform and Pachycaul Succulents by Gordon Rowley is a wonderful book – a well-illustrated and easy-to-read account of these fascinating plants.

Pachypodium and Adenium

Two similar genera of the family *Apocynaceae* from Africa, the Middle East and Madagascar with appealing swollen succulent stems, deciduous leaves and beautiful flowers. The tree-like species *P. lamerei* and *P. geayi* from Madagascar are popular outdoor landscape plants in warm climates, whilst the smaller species make wonderful glasshouse plants.

The one species of adenium, *A. obesum*, has many subspecies and has now been extensively hybridized. With a few exceptions, cultivation is not difficult so long as a minimum temperature of 10°C (50°F) is maintained in winter, when the plants should be rested by keeping them dry. Adeniums need 15°C

TOP: Titanopsis calcarea.

ABOVE: Titanopsis fulleri. Photo: Eddie Harris

173

Pachypodium
namaquanum *in
its natural habitat
in the Richtersveld,
South Africa.* Photo:
Tom Jenkins

(59°F) or more to thrive and then they can be kept in leaf during the winter by being lightly watered. Propagation is usually by seed, which should be sown fresh for best results.

A useful book on these plants is *Pachypodium and Adenium* by Gordon Rowley.

Pachypodium lamerei *in cultivation in California showing its flowering capability.*

Pachypodium saundersii, *the flowers of this easily grown species.*

Pachypodium brevicaule, *the choicest and smallest species in the genus.*

Pachypodium baronii windsori *is unusual for being a red-flowered species.*

Didiereaceae

This plant family is endemic to Madagascar and is perhaps the one most closely related to the family *Cactaceae*. Although some people doubt that they are truly succulent, they respond well to being cultivated in the same way as succulents and so are much prized by hobbyists. Many grow into trees and form the so-called 'spiny forests' of south-east Madagascar, which are under threat of extinction because of charcoal making and cultivation pressures. It is rare to get any of these plants to flower in a small glasshouse since they need to be large before maturing, however, the unusual appearance of the stems and leaves make them popular subjects for the enthusiast. A minimum winter temperature of 10°C (50°F) is suitable for all species when they should be kept dry to encourage them to lose their leaves and rest. Propagation is usually by cuttings or grafting since seed is rarely available.

The booklet *Didiereaceae* by Gordon Rowley is the only English-language publication that covers all aspects of this interesting family.

Didierea madagascariensis *grows into a tree in Madagascar but can also make an unusual pot plant.*

FAR LEFT: Adenium obesum *in flower and showing developing seed horns.*

Dorstenia

A succulent relative of the fig (ficus), where the minute flowers are produced on a disc-like structure called a hypanthodium that can be curiously shaped with bracts around the edges. Some species have succulent stems that are sometimes greatly swollen and a few have an underground caudex. All need warmth in cultivation, a minimum temperature of 15°C (59°F) in winter, and in summer they appreciate a warm, shady place with adequate moisture at the roots. The caudiciform species are difficult and require careful observation of their growing periods which can be unpredictable, so these are only suitable for the experienced grower looking for a challenge. The flowers are often self-fertile and the seeds are expelled explosively from the hypanthodium, which can result in seedlings appearing spontaneously in pots in the near vicinity.

This dorstenia species from Somalia makes an attractive pot plant with its curious flowers. Photo: Tom Jenkins

Dorstenia foetida produces its flowers in large numbers on a disc-like hypanthodium.

Adenia

This genus is a member of the family *Passifloraceae* so not related to the similarly named adenium described earlier. Most are climbers with tendrils but they lack the spectacular flowers of the familiar passion flowers. Instead, the flowers are small and dioecious, that is, only the flowers of one sex appear on each individual, so you need male and female plants to make seeds. The most appealing of the many species are those that form a swollen caudex from which grow stiff or clambering stems with large or insignificant leaves. They all benefit from plenty of root space, which encourages rapid growth of the caudex – it is said that pruning of the stems will also make the caudex grow quicker. Adenias are usually grown from seed but those with thick fleshy stems can be propagated from cuttings, although they will take a long time to make a caudex.

Adenia globosa *makes a large, textured caudex from which the branches grow.*

Dioscorea

A genus of several hundred species including edible yams but with just a few to interest us here. Probably the best loved of all caudex plants is *D. elephantipes* from southern Africa, often seen labelled as *Testudinaria elephantipes*, which used to be collected and imported into Europe as a source of the steroid diosgenin for the manufacture of cortisone.

The hemispherical caudex is covered with irregularly shaped corky tubercles resulting from the expansion of the growing storage organ. Starting in August, one or more shoots appear from near the top of the caudex and grow rapidly. From these, slender twining side-shoots grow outwards and wind themselves round anything they touch, subsequently producing glossy heart-shaped leaves. The small flowers are single sex and dioe-

cious, so two plants are needed to produce fruits containing the winged seeds. The caudex can ultimately get very large and in habitat is reported to reach over 250kg (550lb). In cultivation, seedlings are easily raised and can develop a caudex of some 12cm (5in) in diameter in about five years. The plants should be watered when in leaf, that is from August until April when a minimum temperature of about 5°C (41°F) is adequate for this undemanding plant.

Other species sometimes grown are *D. sylvatica*, also from southern Africa, and *D. macrostachya* from Mexico, which has a flatter caudex and requires more warmth in cultivation.

Dioscorea elephantipes *grows its vines in winter from a large caudex.*

Cyphostemma

A close relative of cissus, this is a member of the family *Vitaceae*, which includes grapes. All the species develop huge swollen branches and trunks that can reach tree-like proportions. The large fleshy leaves are produced from the top of the branches, as are clusters of small flowers followed by fruits that look like small grapes. These very architectural plants are easily cultivated and should be watered in summer when the leaves and flowers appear. A dry winter rest encourages the leaves to fall when a minimum temperature of 10°C (50°F) is adequate. These plants are highly prized by growers, particularly when they reach a large size.

Cyphostemma juttae
*is a succulent member
of the grape family.*

FAR RIGHT: Senecio
rowleyanus *is a
good plant for a
hanging pot.*

Senecio and Othonna

These genera of the family *Compositae* are characterized by their flowers, which actually consist of a mass of small florets. The succulent species are interesting plants for the keen grower, with stems or leaves evolved for water storage, some even developing a caudex. Careful watering all year round with a minimum temperature of 10°C (50°F) in winter is suitable for most species.

Othonnas are particularly choice subjects and can be tricky to cultivate, being sensitive to excess moisture and requiring adherence to a dry summer rest with just an occasional light spray. They should be watered in early autumn when the leaves will grow, and then in early spring, as watering ceases, the leaves will be shed. Their bright flowers are a real bonus in the collection at a time when few plants bloom. Propagation is either from cuttings or seed but these are plants for growers looking for a challenge and the satisfaction that success brings.

The indispensable guide is *Succulent Compositae* by Gordon Rowley.

Senecio haworthii *is remarkable for its leaves, which are thickly covered with white hair.* Photo: John Pilbeam

Othonna clavifolia *is a winter-growing succulent that needs a sunny location.*

Pelargonium and Sarcocaulon

Familiar to gardeners as versatile floriferous plants for hanging baskets and bedding, the genus pelargonium includes many remarkable succulent species, some with succulent stems and others forming a caudex. They present no great difficulty in cultivation and are easily raised from seed, which have a remarkable mechanism for self planting by means of hygroscopic twisting of an appendage to the seed. The flowers bear a resemblance to their hybrid relatives and, although smaller, have a great appeal.

Sarcocaulon, another member of the family *Geraniaceae*, is even more popular with collectors, perhaps because of the bizarre appearance of the succulent stems, which are usually adorned with the thorn-like persistent petioles of the leaves. It cannot be said that they are difficult to cultivate but they are certainly unpredictable, the fleshy stems sometimes staying dormant for more than a year then breaking into leaf and flower regardless of the season. These drought-tolerant plants should be grown

Othonna herrei, *rare in collections, should be grown in winter when it has leaves and flowers.*

Pelargonium longifolium, *a geophytic species.*

179

Pelargonium
quercifolium.
Photo: John Pilbeam

Sarcocaulon paniculinum *has wonderfully hairy leaves and pink flowers.* Photo: Tom Jenkins

Sarcocaulon vanderietii *is slow growing and can come into leaf at any time of year.*

in the sunniest place available and watered when the leaves appear. The delicate flowers are an added bonus and somewhat of a surprise when produced from the often leafless stems.

The recently published *Geophytic Pelargonium* by Charles Craib with its exquisite illustrations certainly does justice to some of these interesting plants.

Pelargonium
rhodanthum. Photo:
John Pilbeam

Cucurbits

The family *Cucurbitaceae*, famous for giving us cucumbers, marrows, pumpkins, melons and many other edible fruits, also includes some genera that have evolved to exist in arid environments by developing a caudex. There are many examples but only a few are regularly encountered in succulent collections. They have limited appeal, probably because the annual growth from the caudex is usually extensive and clambers by means of tendrils untidily around other plants whilst the flowers are insignificant. The genera most likely to be seen in collections are kedrostis, gerrardanthus, momordica, corallocarpus, xerosicyos and zygosicyos. The key to growing these plants is to keep them warm and adequately watered during the growing season, which is usually summer. A winter minimum of 10°C (50°F) is adequate for most while they are resting but a few may require a higher temperature.

Peperomia dolabella, *a window-leafed species with a caudex in habitat near Cajamarca, Peru.*

Xerosycios has a big caudex and long, non-succulent shoots.

Peperomia

Most familiar as houseplants, this genus has over a thousand species, but only a few are considered to be succulent. The most desirable are those species with succulent windowed leaves that come from Peru and southern Ecuador. Also interesting, and more demanding in cultivation, are those that grow an underground caudex to survive dry periods. The flowers of peperomia are individually insignificant, large numbers clustering on the thin rope-like inflorescence. A warm and bright locality with careful watering around the year suits these unusual plants, with a minimum temperature of 15°C (59°F) in winter when the plants should only be lightly watered.

A series of articles by Gordon Rowley in the *Journal of the British Cactus and Succulent Society,* is a useful reference to those peperomias considered succulent.

Avonia

A genus of the family *Portulacaceae* comprising about ten dwarf species that have a distinctive and appealing appearance. The prostrate or partially erect stems are covered with white papery stipules that protect the plants from excess transpiration and trap valuable dew. The pretty flowers are white or pink and appear singly at the ends of the shoots. These plants will often be found labelled as anacampseros, a genus to which they are closely related. Success in cultivation depends on a bright location and careful watering at all times. Propagation is usually from seed, which is slow to raise, but produces charming young plants.

Avonia quinaria alstonii *has a flat caudex and flowers beautifully.* Photo: Tom Jenkins

Peperomia dolabriformis *under bushes near Balsas in Peru.*

Appendix I

Where to Buy Plants, Seeds and Books

There are only a few large companies in the world selling cacti and succulents to the hobby market because the total market size is relatively small, and the retail price is low considering how long it takes to grow a saleable plant. The principal growers, the majority of which are wholesale, make most of their income from sales through the wider horticultural trade to the general public. The enthusiasts' market is served by a large number of small specialist nurseries where sales of cacti and succulents are not the owner's only source of income. There are also a number of amateur growers that sell their spare plants at shows and other events organized by the various cactus societies and specialist study groups. This is particularly true of rarer plants, which are less commercial and have limited appeal (see Appendix II).

A major influence on the trade has been the strengthening of the international regulations controlling the trade in endangered species. The effect has been to greatly reduce the number of habitat-collected plants offered for sale in Europe and the USA. This is very different from the situation that existed until the 1970s where large numbers of habitat-collected specimens were available to collectors – a trade that was very profitable for the importers. Mature plants of slow-growing cactus species, especially those from Mexico, such as ariocarpus, pelecyphora and aztekium, were dug up in their natural habitats to satisfy the demand from collectors around the world. Now we are seeing these species being grown from seed instead, particularly in parts of the world such as California and Mediterranean Europe where the climate allows saleable plants to be grown in a reasonable time.

The seed suppliers usually offer a wide range of species, only some of which will have been produced from their own plants in cultivation. They will often compliment their own stocks of seed with species from other dealers and collectors, who are in a position to obtain seed collected from habitat, or from plants cultured in a more favourable climate where flowering is more easily achieved. The quality of commercially supplied seed can be variable and some species will fail to germinate through no fault of the sowing process. This failure can be due to the seed being stored badly or for too long, but even freshly collected seed will sometimes be useless, perhaps because it was unripe when collected, not effectively pollinated, or for some other reason beyond the control of the supplier. Reputable dealers will usually replace the odd failure.

To find the most up-to-date information, you should visit the Cactus Mall on the internet at www.cactus-mall.com where you will find a list of all the main nurseries, many of them with their own web sites and often with a list of what they have available for sale. There are many nurseries based in the EU and plants may be easily sent between countries now that complicated documentation is no longer required. The favourable climate in southern Europe allows nurseries located there to offer plants that are difficult to propagate in the colder north. Buying plants from nurseries in the USA is difficult if you don't live there. Seed and books, however, can be sent around the world fairly easily although the total number of specialist suppliers around the world is small.

Listed below is a selection of nurseries that will usually supply plants by mail order or sometimes to visitors. This does not constitute a personal recommendation; it is just a list of the better-known suppliers.

Plants

Australia
Hamilton's World of Cacti, Llandilo, NSW
   www.cactus-mall.com/hamilton
Tarrington Exotics, Teesdale, VIC
   www.tarrex.com.au

Germany
Albert Plapp, Jesendorf www.kakteen-plapp.de
Andreae, Otzberg-Lengfeld dandreae@gmx.de
Cono's Paradise, Nettehoefe www.conos-paradise.com
Eden Plants, Erkelenz-Golkrath www.eden-plants.com
Exotica, Erkelenz-Golkrath www.cactus-mall.com/exotica
Gerhard Köhres, Darmstadt koehres@t-online.de
Kakteen Haage, Erfurt www.kakteen-haage.de
Piltz Kakteen, Düren post@kakteen-piltz.de
Uhlig Kakteen, Kernen www.uhlig-kakteen.com

Italy
Botaniké, Baveno (VB) www.botanike.com
Fiore di Cactus, S. Zaccaria (Ravenna) tel: 0544 554084
Fioreverde, Montecchio (RE) fioreverde@tin.it
Il Sole, Brendola (VI) il.sole.piante@libero.it
Paolo Panarotto, S. Giovanni Ilarione (VR) ppanar@tin.it

UK
Abbey Brook Nursery, Matlock, Derbyshire
   tel: 01629 580306
Aristocacti, Bingley, Yorkshire de.quail@virgin.net
Brookside Nursery, New York, Lincolnshire
   alanbutler1@compuserve.com
Chiltern Hills Cacti, Aylesbury, Buckinghamshire
   andy_palmer@chilternhillscacti.freeserve
Chris Rodgerson, Sheffield, Yorkshire
   chris@conophytum.com
Connoisseurs' Cacti, Orpington, Kent
   jp@connoisseurs-cacti.fsnet.co.uk
Croston Cacti, Chorley, Lancashire
   desert.plants@lineone.net
Eau Brink Cactus Nursery, Kings Lynn, Norfolk
   tel: 01553 617635
Glenhirst Cactus Nursery, Boston, Lincolnshire
   info@cacti4u.co.uk
Holly Gate Cactus Nursery, Ashington, West Sussex
   info@hollygatecactus.co.uk
Kent Cacti, Orpington, Kent tel: 01689 836249
Plant Lovers, Spilsby, Lincolnshire tel: 01754 890256
Plantlife, Eastbourne, East Sussex
   stuart@plantlife.freeserve.co.uk
Richard and Wendy Edginton, Norwich, Norfolk
   tel: 01508 470153
Southfields Nursery, Bourne, Lincolnshire
   tel: 01778 570168
Tamarisk Nurseries, Leighton Buzzard, Bedfordshire
   alan@tamarisk-nursery.demon.co.uk
Toobees Exotics, Woking, Surrey
   sales@toobees.com
Whitestone Gardens, Thirsk, North Yorkshire
   roy@whitestn.demon.co.uk

USA
Arid Land Greenhouses, Tucson, AZ
   www.aridlands.com
Bach's Cactus Nursery, Tucson, AZ www.bachs-cacti.com
Bob Smoley's Garden World, Gibsonia, PA
   www.bobsmoleys.com
Burks' Nursery, Benton, AZ
   www.theamateursdigest.com/burks.htm
Cactus Data Plants, Littlerock, CA

www.cactus-mall.com/cactusdataplants
Cactuslands, Tucson, AZ www.cactuslands.com
Exotic Plants, North Hollywood, CA www.RareExotics.com
Grigsby Cactus Gardens, Vista, CA
   www.cactus-mall.com/grigsby
Highland Succulents, Gallipos, OH
   www.highlandsucculents.com
Miles To Go, Cortaro, AZ www.miles2go.com
Rare Plant Research, Portland, OR
   www.theamateursdigest.com/rareplnt.htm
Steven Hammer's Sphaeroid Institute, Vista, CA
   www.cactus-mall.com/rana

Seeds

Andreae, Otzberg-Lengfeld, Germany
   dandreae@gmx.de
Arizona Cactus Garden, Hoppers Crossing, Australia
   viglasky@optusnet.com.au
Cactus Heaven, Mosta, Malta gauci@cactus-heaven.com
DeHerdt Brothers, Rijkevorsel, Belgium tel: (03) 314 6942
Doug and Vivi Rowland, Kempston, Bedfordshire, UK
   tel: 01234 358970
Gerhard Köhres, Darmstadt, Germany koehres@t-online.de
Ludwig Bercht, Eck en Wiel, Holland bercht@nzo.nl
Mesa Garden, Belen, New Mexico, USA cactus@swcp.com
Piltz Kakteen, Düren, Germany post@kakteen-piltz.de
SuccSeed, Skogstorp, Sweden www.succseed.com
Uhlig Kakteen, Kernen, Germany www.uhlig-kakteen.com

Books

Byblos, Baveno (VB), Italy byblos@itweb.it
Dr. Gottfried Gutte, Berlin, Germany
   Dr.G.Gutte@cactusbooks.com
Jörg Köpper, Wuppertal, Germany
   joergkoepper@t-online.de
Licosa, Firenze, Italy licosa@ftbcc.it/licosa
Rainbow Gardens Bookshop, Vista, USA
   orders@rainbowgardensbookshop.com
Uhlig Kakteen, Kernen, Germany www.uhlig-kakteen.com
Whitestone Gardens, Thirsk, North Yorkshire, UK
   roy@whitestn.demon.co.uk

Paradise for the collector – a large range of cacti and succulents for sale in a German nursery.

Appendix II
International Societies and Special Interest Groups

The enjoyment of your hobby will be greatly enhanced by sharing it with others. Joining one of the many societies is the best way to learn about events and take part in activities. You can often get plants from other enthusiasts that are not available from the usual commercial sources. As you become more interested in a particular plant group, you may feel it is worth joining one of the specialist interest groups. They have an international membership and often have seed or plant offers, and the information they publish is not easy to find elsewhere.

The most up-to-date information on all societies and interest groups may be found on www.cactus-mall.com.

International Societies

Czech Republic
Kuktusy
Jan Riha, Pivovarska 861
CZ-289 22 Lysa nad Labem
riha.j@sendme.cz

France
ARIDES Association
Michel Douziech
Le Bois Magné
F-17250 Sainte Gemme
micheldouziech@wanadoo.fr

Germany/Austria/Switzerland
DKG-Geschäftsstelle
Herr Martin Klingel
Oos-Str. 18
D-75179 Pforzheim
Geschaeftsstelle@DeutscheKakteenGesellschaft.de

Italy
AIAS
Luciano Zambianchi
Via Dei Sardi 44
I-00185 Roma
lzambia@tin.it

Mexico
Sociedad Mexicana de Cactologia
Apartado Postal 60-487
San Pedro de los Pinos
03801 México

Netherlands
Succulenta
Banninkstraat 5
7255 AT Hengelo (Gld.)
roozegaa@tref.nl

Peru
Sociedad Peruana de Cactus y
Suculentas (SPECS)
Aptdo. 3215
Lima 100
carlosto@ec-red.com

South Africa
The Succulent Society of South Africa
Private Bag X10
0028 Hatfield
Pretoria
sssa@succulents.net

UK
The British Cactus and Succulent Society
Mr D V Slade
15 Brentwood Crescent
Hull Road
York YO10 5HU
DSlade@bcss.freeserve.co.uk

Sedum Society
Sedum and relatives
pearcy@btinternet.com

Tephrocactus Study Group
South American opuntiods
geissler.w@virgin.net

Other Periodicals

There are two other well-illustrated and recommended journals with English text:

Cactus & Co
Dual language Italian/English with wonderful large pictures
Subscription: Mariangela Costanzo, viale Piave 69, I-20060 Pessano (MI), Italy
E-mail: guppyec@jumpy.it

International Cactus Adventures
English and French editions available
Joël Lode, Desert Springs S.L. Villaricos,
Cuevas del Almanzora, SPAIN (AL)
E-mail: jlcactus@eresmas.net

FAR LEFT: The Dutch Society, Succulenta, promoting the hobby at a large horticultural show.

BELOW: The Chileans, a specialist interest group for South American cacti.

BOTTOM: The International Ascepiad Society caters for those interested in stapeliads and their relatives.

USA
The Cactus and Succulent Society of America
Mindy Fusaro
PO Box 2615
Pahrump
NV 89041-2615
cssa@wizard.com

Special Interest Groups

The following is restricted to English-language groups, but there are many interest groups working in other languages.

UK
Alsterworthia International
Aloe, haworthia, gasteria, bulbine etc.
hmays@freenetname.co.uk

The Chileans
South American cacti
chileans@btinternet.com

The Haworthia Society
Aloe, haworthia, gasteria, bulbine etc.
stirlingbaker@mortgage199.fsnet.co.uk

International Ascepiad Society
Ascepiadaceae and Apocynaceae
alanbutler@compuserve.com

International Sansevieria Society
Sansevieria and Dracaenaceae
michaelphillips8@btinternet.com

Mammillaria Society
Mammillaria, thelocactus, coryphantha etc.
mammsoc@utiadv.demon.co.uk

The Mesemb Study Group
Mesembryanthemaceae
msg@cactus-mall.com

185

Appendix III

Further Reading and Reference

There are relatively few primary reference works on succulents, so when a new book appears and becomes the leading authority on a subject, it can soon be out of print. You should be able to find most of the books listed here in the library of your local BCSS branch, your public library or as second-hand copies for sale. Some of the older reference books are, however, rare and may take some finding, but are well worth the search.

Recommended specialist texts for further information, organized by the chapters in this book:

Chapter 1
Classification & Nomenclature
Hunt, D. CITES *Cactaceae Checklist*, 2nd Edition (RBGK 1999)
Rowley, G. D., *Name that Succulent*, (Stanley Thornes Ltd, 1980)
History
Rowley, G. D., *A History of Succulent Plants* (Strawberry Press, 1997)

Chapter 2
Succulents in Habitat
Cowling, R. & Pierce, S., *Namaqualand. A Succulent Desert* (Fernwood Press, 1999)
Herm, K. et al., *Cacti in Brazil* (self-published, 2001)
Mauseth, J., Kiesling, R. & Ostolaza, C., *A Cactus Odyssey* (Timber Press, 2002)
Preston-Mafham, K., *Cacti and Succulents in Habitat* (Cassell, 1994)
New Discoveries
Eggli, U. & Taylor, N.P., *IOS Index of Names of Cactaceae published 1950–1990* (RBGK, ZSS, 1991)
Eggli, U. & Taylor, N.P., *List of Names of*

Succulent Plants published 1950–1992 (RBGK, ZSS, 1994)
Field Numbers
Chileans, *Compendium of Field Number Lists* (The Chileans, 1996)

Chapter 3
Shows
BCSS, *Handbook of Shows, 8th Edition* (BCSS, 1997)
Culture
Buxbaum, F., *Cactus Culture Based on Biology* (Blandford Press, 1958)

Chapter 4
Copiapoa
Charles, G., *Copiapoa* (Cirio Publishing Services Ltd, 1998)
Schulz, R. & Kapitany, A., *Copiapoa in their Environment* (Schulz Publishing, 1996)
Coryphantha
Dicht, R. & Lüthy, A., *Coryphantha* (Ulmer-Verlag, 2003)
Discocactus
Buining, A., *Discocactus* (Succulenta, 1980)
Echinocereus
Blum et al., *Echinocereus* (self-published, 1998)
Di Martino, L., *Echinocereus Special* (Cactus & Co., 1996)
Taylor, N. P., *Echinocereus* (RBGK/Collingridge, 1985)
Echinopsis
Rausch, W., *Lobivia* (Rudolf Herzig, 1975)
Rausch, W.,) *Lobivia '85* (Rudolf Herzig, 1985
Epiphytic Cacti
Leue, M., *Epiphyllum* (self-published, 1987)
McMillan, A. J. S. & Horobin, J. F., *Christmas Cacti* (Succulent Plant Research, 1995)
Eriosyce

Katterman, F., *Eriosyce* (Succulent Plant Research, 1994)
Gymnocalycium
Pilbeam, J., *Gymnocalycium, A Collectors' Guide* (A. A. Balkema, 1995)
Mammillaria
Pilbeam, J., *Mammillaria* (Cirio Publishing Services Ltd, 1999)
Matucana
Bregman, R., *The genus Matucana* (A. A. Balkema, 1996)
Melocactus
Taylor, N. P., 'The genus Melocactus in Central and South America', *Bradleya 9* (BCSS, 1991)
Mexican Treasures
Anderson et al., *Threatened Cacti of Mexico* (Succulent Plant Research, 1994)
Pilbeam, J., *Ariocarpus etc.* (2003)
Parodia
Gerloff et al., *Notokakteen* (Kleten-Verlag, 1995)
Mace, T., *Notocactus* (1980)
Rebutia
Pilbeam, J., *Rebutia*, (Cirio Publishing Services Ltd, 1997)
Pilbeam, J., *Sulcorebutia and Weingartia. A Collector's Guide* (Batsford, 1985)
Stenocactus
Taylor, N. P., 'A Commentary on the genus Echinofossulocactus Lawr', *Cactus & Succulent Journal of Great Britain Vol 41(2) 35–42* (1979)
Thelocactus
Mosco, A. & Zanovello, C., 'Thelocactus', *Cactus & Co Vol.6(3) 144–171* (2002)
Pilbeam, J., *Thelocactus* (Cirio Publishing Services Ltd, 1996)
Uebelmannia
Schulz, R. & Machado, M., *Uebelmannia and their Environment* (Schulz Publishing, 2000)

Chapter 5
Agavaceae
Chahinian, B. Juan, *Sansevieria Trifasciata Varieties* (1986)
Gentry, H. S., *Agaves of Continental North America* (University of Arizona Press, 1982)
Irish, M. & G., *Agaves, Yuccas and Related Plants* (Timber Press, 2000)
Crassulaceae
Pilbeam, J., Rodgerson, C. & Tribble, D., *Adromischus* (Cirio Publishing Services Ltd, 1998)

Rowley, G. D., *Crassula* (Cactus & Co., 2003)
Euphorbiaceae
Euphorbia Journal Vols 1–10 (Strawberry Press, 1983–96)
Liliaceae
Bayer, B., *Haworthia Revisited* (Umdaus Press, 1999)
Van Jaarsveld, E., *Gasterias of South Africa* (Fernwood Press, 1994)
Van Wyk, B.-E. & Smith, G., *Guide to the Aloes of South Africa* (Briza Publications, 1996)
Mesembryanthemaceae
Hammer, S., *Dumpling and his Wife [Conophytum]* (EAE Creative Colour Ltd, 2002)
Hammer, S., *Lithops – Treasures of the Veld* (BCSS, 1999)
Various Authors, *Mesembs of the World* (Briza Publications, 1998)
Miscellaneous Succulents
Craib, C., *Geophytic Pelargoniums* (Umdaus Press, 2001)
Rowley, G. D., *Caudiciform and Pachycaul Succulents* (Strawberry Press, 1987)
Rowley, G. D., *Didiereaceae* (BCSS, 1992)
Rowley, G. D., *Pachypodium and Adenium* (Cirio Publishing Services Ltd, 1999)
Rowley, G. D., *Succulent Compositae* (Strawberry Press, 1994)

Classic Reference Books about Cacti
Anderson, E. F., *The Cactus Family* (Timber Press, 2001)
Backeberg, C., *Die Cactaceae* (6 volumes) (Gustav Fischer, 1958–62)
Backeberg, C., *The Cactus Lexicon* (Blandford, 1977)
Benson, L., *The Cacti of the United States and Canada* (Stanford University Press, 1982)
Borg, J., *Cacti* (Macmillan, then Blandford, 1937 and later editions)
Britton, N. L. & Rose, J. N., *The Cactaceae* (4 volumes) (Carnegie Institute, 1919–23 and later editions)
Krainz, H., *Die Kakteen* (63 parts) (Franckhische Verlagshandlung, 1956–75)
Ritter, F., *Kakteen in Südamerika* (4 volumes) (self-published, 1979–81)
Schumann, K., *Gesamtbeschreibung der Kakteen* (J. Neumann, 1899 and later editions)

Selected Reference Books about Other Succulents
Court, D., *Succulent Flora of Southern Africa* (A. A. Balkema, 1981 & 2000)

Eggli, U., *Illustrated Handbook of Succulent Plants* (6 volumes) (Springer, 2001–3)

Herre, H., *The Genera of the Mesembryanthemaceae* (Tafelberg-Uitgewers Beperk, 1971)

Jacobsen, H., *A Handbook of Succulent Plants* (3 volumes) (Blandford, 1960)

Jacobsen, H., *Lexicon of Succulent Plants* (Blandford, 1974 and later editions)

Rauh, W., *Succulent and Xerophytic Plants of Madagascar* (2 volumes) (Strawberry Press, 1995–8)

Reynolds, G. W., *The Aloes of Southern Africa* (The Aloes Book Fund, 1950 and later editions)

Reynolds, G. W., *The Aloes of Tropical Africa and Madagascar* (The Aloes Book Fund, 1966)

Rowley, G. D., *The Illustrated Encyclopedia of Succulents* (Salamander, 1978)

White, A. & Sloane, B. L., *The Stapelieae* (Abbey Garden Press, 1937)

White, A., Dyer, A. & Sloane, B. D., *The Succulent Euphorbieae* (Abbey Garden Press, 1941)

Serial Publications

A tremendous amount of useful information about plants and cultivation, as well as most of the first descriptions of new discoveries, is published in the various specialist journals around the world. The majority of these are published by cactus and succulent societies, so to subscribe you usually join the relevant society, but there are a few that are available in the same way as books, for example yearbooks.

The following are leading journals and yearbooks, including some that have now ceased publication but are often available second hand. The language is English unless otherwise indicated.

Yearbooks and Special Publications

Bradleya, yearbook of the British Cactus & Succulent Society, published yearly since 1983

Haseltonia, yearbook of the Cactus & Succulent Society of America, published since 1993

Schumannia, occasional special publication of the German Society (DKG), three issues published up to 2002 (German with some English translations)

Journals

Aloe, journal of the South African Aloe and Succulent Society, published since 1963

British Cactus & Succulent Journal, published by the British Society (BCSS) since 1983

Cactaceas y Suculentas Mexicanas, journal of the Mexican Society, published since 1955 (in Spanish)

Cactus (Paris), journal of the French Association des Amateurs de Cactées et Plantes Grasses, published from 1946 to 1967; all issues are rare

Cactus Adventures, journal of the French Society ARIDES, English edition published since 1996

Cactus & Co, open-sale journal published in Italy since 1997 (in Italian and English)

Cactus & Succulent Journal of Great Britain, published by the C. & S. Society of Great Britain from 1932 to 1982

Desert Plant Life, open-sale journal published from 1929 until 1952 in California, USA

Excelsa, journal of the Aloe, C. & S. Society of Zimbabwe, published since 1971

Kakteen und andere Sukkulenten, journal of the German Society (DKG), published under various names since 1891; early issues are very rare (in German)

Kaktusy, Journal of the Czech Society, published since 1965 (in Czech)

National Cactus & Succulent Journal (UK), published by the National C. & S. Society from 1946 to 1982

Piante Grasse, journal of the Italian Society AIAS (in Italian)

Quepo, journal of the Peruvian Society, published since 1987 (in Spanish)

Succulenta, journal of the Dutch Society, published since 1919 (in Dutch)

Succulentes, journal of the French Society AIAPS, published since 1977 (in French)

The Internet

The most useful source of up-to-date information is now the internet. It has provided a cheap, readily accessed medium for people who have a minority interest to publish their pictures and text. The easiest way to find information about cacti and other succulents is to go to www.cactus-mall.com, maintained in the UK by Dr Tony Mace, where you will find multi-lingual links to related sites all over the world. At the time of writing, the following is a selection of what you can find on the Cactus Mall: clubs and societies; nurseries; news; book publishers and dealers; The Cactus and Succulent Bookshop; cactus and succulent indexes and services.

Appendix IV
Glossary of Terms

Actinomorphic Radially symmetric, applied to flowers that are symmetrical about any plane.
Anther Part of the stamen that produces the pollen.
Appressed Flattened against the stem.
Areole A highly modified short shoot unique to cacti, from which flowers and offsets arise. It is usually a felty cushion with spines or hairs growing out of it.
Axil The depression between the tubercles of a mammillaria from where the flowers appear.
BCSS British Cactus and Succulent Society.
Bract A modified petal, usually small and at the base of a flower, but can be large and brightly coloured as with some euphorbias.
Caatinga Deciduous woodland in north-east Brazil with pronounced dry periods.
Cactus A plant belonging to the plant family *Cactaceae*.
CAM Crassulacean Acid Metabolism. A modified assimilation process found mainly in succulent plants.
Caudex A general term for the swollen part of a succulent used for water storage, which can be a stem or a root.
Caudiciform A plant with a caudex, above or below ground, used for storage of water.
Central spine One of the innermost spines of the areole.
Cephalium A modified part of some species of cactus solely for the production of flowers and fruits, usually comprising dense hair or bristles.
CITES Convention on International Trade in Endangered Species.
Cleistogamous Describes flowers that do not open but are capable of producing fruit with viable seed.
Cristate A form of abnormal growth in the shape of a fan, a crest.
Cultivar A propagated strain of a plant developed or selected in cultivation.
Decumbent Creeping along the ground with the stem tip raised.
Dehiscent The natural opening or splitting of a fruit when ripe.
Dichotomous Branching into two equal branches.
Dicotyledon Flowering plants which usually have two seed leaves upon germination.
Dioecious Each flower has only male or female parts, and each individual only bears flowers of one sex.
Distichous Arrangement of leaves or branches in two opposite rows.
Endemic Having a limited or localized distribution.
Epidermis The outermost protective layer of cells of the stem or leaf.
Epiphyte A plant that grows on another plant using it for support but not obtaining any nutrient from it.
Geophyte With much of the plant below ground, often with a thickened root or caudex.
Glochids Tiny barbed spines that easily become detached and often occur in tufts. They are unique to opuntia relatives.
Growing-point The cells at the tip of a shoot or root that are capable of division to produce new tissue.

Inflorescence A cluster of flowers.
IOS International Organisation for Succulent Plant Study.
Monocotyledon Flowering plants which usually have a single seed leaf upon germination.
Monoecious Each flower has only male or female parts, and each individual bears flowers of both sexes.
Offset A side-shoot that can be detached for propagation.
Pectinate In the shape of a comb, radiating from along a straight line.
Plumose Feathery, a structure having fine hairs attached to the sides, e.g. some spines.
Pubescent Covered in fine hair.
Radial spine One of the outermost of the spines of an areole, which are usually radiating or appressed.
Rotate Shaped like a wheel, describes flowers where the petals are symmetrically disposed like the spokes of a wheel.
Self-fertile Able to produce fertile seed having been pollinated with its own pollen.
Self-sterile Unable to produce viable seed or any seed from pollination using its own pollen.
Solitary An undivided stem, singular.
ssp Subspecies, the next taxonomic division below species, now preferred in the *Cactaceae*.
Stamen The pollen-bearing male part of the flower.
Stigma The female part of the flower that receives the pollen.
Stolon A runner or sucker, a basal branch just above or below the soil that can give rise to new plantlets.
Stomata Minute pores in the epidermis through which gases can pass.
Succulent A drought-adapted plant with the ability to store water in specialist tissues.
Synonym A plant name that has been replaced by another, due to greater understanding of relationships leading to a new nomenclature.
Taxon A general term for any taxonomic category, e.g. species or genus.
Taxonomy The study of the classification of organisms.
Testa The outer protective layer of a seed, the seed coat.
Tuber Enlarged underground part of a stem.
Tubercle A cylindrical or conical outgrowth on a stem, usually bearing part or all of an areole.
Tuberous Shaped like a tuber but often used to describe enlarged roots.
Turgid Filled with water.
Valid Name One published in accordance with the rules of the International Code of Botanical Nomenclature.
Vascular bundle A group of conducting channels through which sap passes along a stem.
X Symbol used to indicate a hybrid.
Xerophyte A plant adapted to an environment with little precipitation, of which succulence is one example.
Zygomorphic Bilaterally symmetrical, applied to flowers where there is only one plane about which the flower is symmetrical.

Index

Italic page numbers indicate an illustration.

Index